"I Will Build My Church!"

"And the Gates of Hell Shall Not Prevail Against It!"

Rudi Louw

Most Scripture quotations are taken from the RSV®, *Revised Standard Version*, Copyright © 1983 by Thomas Nelson, Inc.

Some Scripture quotations were taken from the NKJV, *New King James Version*, Copyright © 1983 by Thomas Nelson, Inc.

The Scripture quotations not taken from the RSV, and NKJV are a *literal translation* of the Scriptures.

The Holy Scriptures are just that, HOLY.

Statements enclosed in brackets were inserted into Scripture quotations to add emphasis or to clarify the meaning of what is being said in those scriptures.

The integrity of God's Word to man was not compromised in any way. Due care and diligence was cautiously exercised to keep the Word of Truth intact.

Content

The Marvel of the Holy Bible

1. Uninterrupted Theme and Inspired Thought

It took *1,500 years* to compile the Holy Bible, involving *more than 40 different authors*. Yet the theme and inspired thought of Scripture, continues *uninterrupted* from author to author, from beginning till end.

2. Absence of Mythical Stories

Compare philosophies and theories about creation in the Middle East, Europe, Asia, Africa, and Latin America and you'll find mythical scenarios: gods feuding and cutting up other gods to form the heavens and the earth, etc.

In ancient Greek mythology, the Greeks see Atlas carrying the earth on his shoulders. In India, Hindus believe eight elephants carry the earth on their backs.

But in contrast, Job, the oldest book in the Holy Bible, declares that, *"God suspends the earth 'on nothing."(Job 26:7)*

This was said millennia before Isaac Newton discovered the invisible laws of gravity that delicately balance every planet and sun in its individual circuit.

Contrary to every other ancient attempt to give a creation account, *the Holy Bible pictures the creation of the earth in a very scientific manner.*

Example: In Genesis Chapter One, the continents are lifted from the seas then vegetation is formed and later animal life all reproducing *'according to its own kind'*, **thus recognizing the fixed genetic laws.** In addition, we have the bringing forth of man and woman, *all done by God in a dignified and proper manner, without mythological adornments.*

The balance or remainder of the Holy Bible follow suite.

The narratives are **true historical documents***, faithfully reflecting society and culture* **as history and archaeology would discover them thousands of years later. Not only is the Holy Bible historically accurate, it is also reliable when it deals with scientifically reliable subjects.**

It was never intended to be a textbook on history, science, mathematics, or medicine. *However, when its writers touch on these subjects, **they often state facts that scientific advancement would not reveal, or even consider, until thousands of years later.***

While many have doubted the accuracy of the Holy Bible, time and continued research have consistently demonstrated that the Word of God is better informed than its critics.

3. Intactness

Of all the ancient works of substantial size, *the Holy Bible survives intact, against all odds and expectations.*

Compared with other ancient writings, the Holy Bible has more manuscripts as evidence to support it than any ten pieces of classical literature combined!

The plays of William Shakespeare, for instance, were written about four hundred years ago, after the invention of the printing press. Many of his original writings and words have been lost in numerous sections, *yet the Holy Bible's uncanny preservation, has weathered thousands of years of wars, contradictions, persecutions, fires and invasions.*

Through the centuries Jewish scribes have preserved the Holy Bible's Old Covenant text, **such as no other manuscripts has ever been preserved. They kept tabs on every letter, syllable, word and paragraph.** *They continued from generation to generation to appoint and train special groups of men within their culture,* **whose sole duty it was to preserve and transmit these documents, <u>with perfect accuracy and fidelity</u>.**

Who ever bothered to count the letters, syllables, or words of Plato, Aristotle, or Seneca for that matter?

When it comes to the New Testament, the actual number of preserved manuscripts is so great that it becomes overwhelming. ***There are more than 5,680 Greek manuscripts, more than 10,000 Latin Vulgate manuscripts and at least 9,300 other versions. Further still, there exists an additional 25,000 manuscript copies of portions of the New Testament.*** **No other document of antiquity even begins to approach such numbers.**

The closest in comparison is Homer's <u>Iliad</u>, with only 643 manuscripts. The first complete work of Homer only dates back to the 13th century.

4. Unmatched Accuracy in Predictive Foretelling

The Holy Bible is unmatched in accuracy in predictive foretelling. No other ancient work even begins to attempt this.

Other books, such as the Koran, the Book of Mormon, and parts of the Veda claim divine inspiration; *but none of these books contain predictive foretelling.*

This one undeniable fact we know for certain: *While microscopic scrutiny would show up the imperfections, blemishes and defects of any work of man, <u>it magnifies the beauties and perfection of God</u>. Just as every flower displays in accurate detail the reflection and perfection of beauty, <u>so does the Word of Truth when it is scrutinized</u>.*

Historian Philip Schaff wrote:

"Without money and weapons, Jesus the Christ conquered more millions, than Alexander, Caesar, Mohammed, and Napoleon. Without science and learning, He (Jesus the Christ) shed more light on things human and divine than all philosophers and scholars combined. Without the eloquence of schools, He (Jesus the Christ) spoke such words of life as was never spoken before or since and produced effects which lie beyond the reach of orator or poet. Without writing a single line, He (Jesus the Christ) set more pens in motion and furnished themes for more sermons, orations, discussions, learned volumes, works of art,

9

*and songs of praise **than the whole army of great men of ancient and modern times combined**." (The Person of Christ,* p33. 1913)

Today, there are literally billions of Bibles in more than 2,000 languages.

Isn't it about time you find out what it really has to say?

Hey listen, the Holy Bible is all about Jesus, the Messiah, the Christ...

...and everything about Jesus Christ is really about YOU!!

Study Tips:

Read 2 Corinthians 5:14, 16, 18, 19, and 21.

In the light of these Scriptures, it should be obvious that, if you want to study the Holy Bible, *you should study it in the light of mankind's redemption!*

Feed daily on redemption realities found in the book of Acts, in Romans Chapters One through Eight, and in Ephesians, Colossians, and Galatians, also in 1 Peter Chapter One, 2 Peter Chapter One, James Chapter 1, as well as in 1 and 2 Corinthians.

Acknowledgement

I want to acknowledge and thank one of my mentors in the faith, Francois du Toit, for blessing and impacting me with revelation knowledge.

I borrowed the portion on *"The Marvel of the Holy Bible"* from his website: http://www.mirrorword.net as students so often feel they have a right to do with things that come from teachers they respect. Just as Galatians 6:6 says: *"Let him who is taught the Word **share in all good things** with him who teaches."*

To all our dear friends and family, and to all those who helped me with this project:

Especially to my wife, Carmen;

For all the love and support, and for keeping me real by being my partner in building Jesus' Church,

THANK YOU!

I love and appreciate you so very much

Foreword

Thank you for taking the time to read this book.

Let me start off by saying that *I am totally addicted to my Daddy's love for me.*

I am in love with Jesus Christ, *and that is enough for me!*

The love of God is so much more than a doctrine, a philosophy, or a theory. It is so much more and goes so much deeper than knowledge: *it way surpasses knowledge.*

We are talking heart language here.

Therefore, this book was not written to impress intellectuals with knowledge and philosophy or theologians with theories and doctrine. Nor was it written to impress English majors with grammar and spelling for that matter.

So, if you do come up with any other definitions or find any language inaccuracies, please don't use it to disqualify Love's own message I bring to you in this book.

I write *to impact people's hearts,* to make them see the mysteries that have been hidden in

Father God's heart concerning Christ Jesus, and really *concerning THEM.* I do this so as to arrest their conscience with it, *that I may introduce them to their original design and their true selves,* **presenting them to themselves perfect in Christ Jesus,** *and setting them apart unto Him* **in love,** *as a chaste virgin.*

We are involved with the biggest romance of the ages!

Therefore, this book cannot be read as you would a novel: *casually.* It is not a cleverly devised little myth or fable. **It contains revelation and** *truth* **about some things you may or may not have considered before.**

It is the TRUTH of God, ultimate TRUTH, and therefore has direct bearing upon YOUR life. **The Word and the Spirit are my witness** *to the reality of these things!*

Be like the people of Berea whom the Apostle Paul ministered to in Acts 17:11. Open yourself up to study the revelation contained in this book, *to see if these things are* **true and real***.*

Be forewarned, and do not become guilty of the sins of the Pharisees, **or you too will miss out on the depth of fulfillment God Himself, who is LOVE, wants to give** <u>**YOU**</u>*.*

Jesus said of the Pharisees and Sadducees that they strain out every little gnat BUT swallow whole camels. What He meant by that is that *some people seem to have it all together when it comes to doctrine and they love to argue.*

It makes them feel important but it is nothing other than EMPTY religious and intellectual pride.

They know the Scriptures in and out and YET they are still so IGNORANT about **REAL TRUTH that is only found in LOVE.**

They are still so ignorant and indifferent **towards the things that REALLY MATTER.**

They are always arguing over the use of *every little jot and tittle* and over the meaning and interpretation of *every word of Scripture.*

The exact thing they accuse everyone else of doing though, the precise thing they judge everyone else for, *they are actually doing themselves.* That is, **they often completely misinterpret and twist what is being said, *making a big deal of insignificant things, while obscuring or weakening God's real truth: the truth of His LOVE.***

They are always majoring on minors **<u>because they do not understand the heart of God</u>**, *and therefore they constantly miss the whole point of the message.*

Paul himself said it so beautifully:

*"…the letter kills but **the Spirit BRINGS LIFE…"***

*"…<u>knowledge puffs up</u>, but **LOVE EDIFIES…"***

I say again:

Allow yourself to get caught up in the revelation I am about to share.

Open yourself up to study the insight contained in this book, *not only with a desire to gain knowledge, but also with anticipation **to hear from Father God yourself, to encounter Him through His Word, and to embrace truth in order to know and believe the LOVE God has for <u>you.</u>***

*Get so caught up in it **that you too may receive from Him LOVE'S impartation of LIFE.***

*If you take heed to these things and yield yourself fully to it, **it is custom designed and guaranteed to forever alter and enrich your life!***

16

"Who do men say that the son
of man is?"

"And they said,
'Some say
John the Baptist,
others say
Elijah,
and others
Jeremiah
or one of the prophets.'"

"But who do you say that I am?"

"Simon Peter replied,
'You are the Christ,
the Son of the living God."

"And Jesus answered him,
'Blessed are you,
Simon Bar-Jona!
For flesh and blood
has not revealed this to you,

but my Father who is in
heaven.'

'And I tell you, **you are Peter**

…and **on this rock I will build
my church**

…and the powers of death
shall not prevail against it.

I will give you the keys of the
kingdom of heaven

. . .and whatever you bind on earth shall be bound in heaven

. . .and whatever you loose on earth shall be loosed in heaven.'

~ Matthew 16:13-19

Chapter 1

Judah Shall Plow

Turn with me in your Bible to Matthew Chapter Sixteen. If you do not have your Bible available then just keep reading. Jesus said in Verse Eighteen,

"I tell you, you are Peter, and upon this rock I will build My 'church'."

"...upon this rock I will build My 'church'!"

In the context of this statement, Jesus earlier began to challenge His disciples to see what they would say. Jesus asked the question,

"Who do men say the son of man is?"

It's so easy to realize from their answers that every person had an opinion about Jesus. I mean, Jesus had such a remarkable ministry that no one could ignore Him. But it is also quite obvious that people were, and still are, so very confused when it comes to this subject of, not only the identity of Jesus, but the identity of man period.

So, people had differing opinions about Him, but then Jesus began to challenge His own disciples and He asks them directly,

"But who do you say that I am?"

And it was then that Peter blurted out,

"You are the Christ, the Son of the living God!"

Peter apparently came up with the correct answer. And Jesus then said,

"Blessed are you Simon, Bar-Jona…"

Meaning, *"Blessed are you Simon, son of Jona."*

So, Jesus made reference to Simon's earthly father.

He said: *"Blessed are you…"*

"For flesh and blood did not reveal this to you."

In other words, *"You did not get this from flesh and blood. You did not get this from a natural identity or from your earthly father,"*

He says, *"…but my heavenly Father **revealed** this to you."*

In other words, *"My heavenly Father **gave birth to this revelation, in your heart!**"*

He basically said, *"This is not a revelation that you received **after the flesh** (or from the flesh, or by the flesh; from any fleshly identity)."*

*"But you received it **through an impartation!**"*

*"You received it through an impartation **from my heavenly Father!**"*

And He says, *"Listen, I tell you, you are Peter!"*

"Your father calls you Simon, but because of this impartation, because of this revelation, I give you a new name, a new identity. I call you Peter!"

You see, the world calls Jesus all kinds of things. They give Him all kinds of funny names and call Him all kinds of things because they have a certain idea of who they think Jesus would be, and who they think He should be.

But when the Father revealed His Son, He revealed Him for who He really is, and so, when the Father reveals Jesus' true identity to your heart, something is given birth to within your spirit. Something is born within you: *a revelation!*

And then He's no longer a swearword. He's no longer some distant, historic figure. But He becomes to you the Son, the Christ, the Messiah, the anointed one of God, and He becomes to you what He truly is.

In that moment He also changes *your* identity!

Maybe in the past, you were what you were according to the flesh, but when He reveals your true identity to you, you are that other person no longer, because you no longer know yourself according to the flesh. That identity no longer applies to you.

And maybe we just need to quickly turn to Hosea Chapter Ten. I read something very interesting there in Hosea 10:12,

"Sow for yourselves righteousness, and reap the fruit of steadfast love. Break up your fallow ground, for it is the time to seek the Lord that He may come and rain salvation upon you."

Now, before the rain comes, there must be some plowing, but look at Verse Eleven.

Verse 11 says, *"Judah shall plow and Jacob must harrow for himself."*

He says, *"I will put Ephraim to the yoke..."*

You see, God wants to rain salvation upon the earth. God wants to literally saturate the soil of the earth with the blessing of His love, the blessing of His salvation, with the blessing of the liberty which comes through His Word, *through the truth of the gospel.* But the soil must yield to the plow. **There must be some plowing up of old ideas.**

It doesn't benefit someone who wants to become a farmer to just sit on the porch with his hands in his pockets thinking, *'Wow, it is going to be so wonderful when these fields are full of corn ripening on the stalk as far as the eye can see. And it is going to be so great, because I am going to get such a bountiful harvest, and then I am going to be such a rich man!'*

Listen, that farmer is going to have to take his hands out of his pockets and do some plowing to prepare the soil for the seed. And then he is going to have to watch over that seed and fertilize it and water it and whatever it takes, until the full harvest comes forth. If he doesn't do these things he can come and have the best seed sown into his fields, but the seed will be wasted.

I have personally seen so often how so many people can sit and listen and hear the same message, the truth of the gospel, the very Word of God, without receiving the full revelation of it. They never get the full conclusion, the full life-transforming impact and effect of the Word.

They can even sit here, reading the same book as you, but they will sit there, all distracted with this and distracted with that, and the seed will be wasted on them. That seed will not produce what it was meant to produce in their lives.

"Judah shall plow…"

The word *"Judah"* means: **praise.**

Praise is an estimation of value term.

The word praise also means: to price.

Therefore you will praise or put a price on whatever you value.

Whenever you discover the value of something *it will take on worth to you* and therefore some things we value are priceless to us. That means it is so valuable that you cannot even begin to put a price on it. The word *'appreciation'* comes to mind.

You see, praise, or appreciation, creates an atmosphere that breaks through the realm of the spirit so that the kingdom of Jesus can be established within us, in our midst, among us and through us.

Whenever we gather together *as believers* – even in this book we are gathering together, amen – so whenever we gather together, we gather to declare in the spirit realm the Lordship of Jesus within us and over us.

You see, we are not just a bunch of bodies gathering together and sitting there, a bunch of meat and bones etc. And here we are, sitting, and trying to get comfortable for an hour or two. No, we are spirits. We came in our bodies, and our bodies are like our automobiles, they brought us to wherever we are gathering. It's like a vehicle and it takes us places and it took you to that chair or that couch or whatever it is you are sitting on or in.

But we are spirits and we brought our spirits into that place where we gather and where we meet. And we have come together to submit our spirits to the Holy Spirit. We have come to submit our spirits to the government of the Spirit of God, amen.

Our praises are simply a recognition. When we get together in praise and worship, we vocally express our recognition of the Lordship of the government of Jesus Christ. We declare that Jesus is in dominion and that He reigns within us. You see, God is omnipresent, but when we begin to acknowledge and recognize and declare His Lordship and His praises, *He manifests Himself to us and within,* **and in the manifestation of His presence He breaks the powers of darkness.**

Almost every time we gather together and come together for fellowship and for the praise and worship of Jesus, there are inevitably people in that place of fellowship with us that have come with some real serious need in their lives and they have come up against a wall of some circumstance and they don't know how to break through. Maybe they are trapped in some addiction or some sickness or some other power of darkness and they don't know how to break loose, how to break free.

But let me assure you, you have come to the right place of fellowship in reading this book.

As you read this book with a desire to encounter God, your spirit not only engages my spirit in this book, but your spirit also engages God, because there is liberty in this book because of the Word that is preached!

You will engage and know the truth and the truth will set you free!

And God will perform miracles whenever we gather together, yes even as you and I are gathering together in this book. He will perform miracles like only He alone can do *because He confirms His Word. He confirms the truth of the gospel with signs and wonders following!*

In fact, you can even receive a miracle right now. I want to say to you that as you get together with the saints, and as we connect in this book, I want you, consciously, to draw your attention to the Father, and to give Him the praise of your heart, and to respect and honor His nearness and His very presence, amen.

"Judah shall plow..."

28

"Sow for yourselves righteousness, and reap the fruit of steadfast love. Break up your fallow ground, for it is the time to seek the Lord that He may come and rain salvation upon you."

It's time to seek the Lord, amen. *Not Men,* but the Lord, amen.

Father, we've come to seek Your face. We've come to present ourselves before You, as a living sacrifice.

And Father, we are plowing our hearts wide open, we are plowing, and we are presenting to You good soil, Father, the good soil of a yielded heart.

Father, let the seed of Your Word, the seed of Your gospel, let it fall into our hearts, let it sink in deep …deep enough Father.

…And Father, let your Spirit then also rain salvation upon us.

In Jesus Name.

Amen.

Chapter 2

Our Identity in Him

Let's get back to Matthew Chapter Sixteen.

Peter replied, *"You are the Christ, the Son of the living God."*

Jesus said, *"Blessed are you, Simon, son of Jona..."*

"...for flesh and blood has not revealed this to you;"

"...but My Father who is in heaven."

"And I tell you, you are Peter."

Can you see that the minute Peter acknowledged who Jesus really was, *his whole identity was changed!*

He discovered who *he* really was, from God's eternal perspective, from God's value of him as God's child, Jesus revealed it to him.

Isn't that amazing?!

When I discover Jesus for who He really is,
He shows me who I really am.

In that discovery of Jesus, and who He really is, He gives me a new identity. I am no longer a **simion** – like a reed, you know, just following and leaning towards whatever direction the wind is blowing. But instead He gives me a new identity. He makes me a **petros** – a rock. Steadfast and immovable, secure as secure can be. *Secure in my new identity as God's child, secure in my sonship, I have discovered in Him.*

And He says, *"Upon this rock (Upon this discovery, upon this revelation, upon this mutual sonship; upon this **identity revealed** in Him)..."*

He says, *"Upon this rock, I will build my 'church'..."*

Now listen, we can't afford to look at the natural and think that it is upon saint Peter that God's building His 'church'.

God is building His 'church' upon this foundation: **the revelation of Christ.**

God's revelation of the true identity of Christ, and therefore God's revelation of you in Christ, and Christ in you; *that whole original, authentic identity of us as children of God revealed and restored in Christ,* that is the rock solid revelation and foundation that God is building His *'church'* upon.

Christ revealed to be in you; *Christ in you* is the hope of glory, amen.

(Note: The word *'church'* is actually the word **ekklesia.** It is a combination of two words: **ek** *and* **klesia. Klesia** *comes from the root word* **kaleo.** Thus: **ek** – which always denotes origin. It means to come out of or proceed from, and **kaleo** – which means to call by name, to identify, to surname.

Thus the word *'church'* does not refer to a building or an organization; it refers to our joint sonship with Jesus; to our authentic original identity restored to us as genuine children of God.

The word *'church'* or *'ekklesia,'* refers to those who have been called out by name to discover or know their true identity according to their origin. *They have been given a name or an identity by the One who is their origin.*

They have been identified and surnamed by Christ. Christ claimed them as members of His household, carrying the same name, the same identity, *because they share the same origin.* He is not ashamed to call us His brethren; to refer to us as children of God. (See Hebrews 2:11))

I say again, **God is building HIS *'church'*
upon the revelation of Christ, upon THIS
knowledge of HIS identity *and our identity
in Him as children of God revealed and
restored.* God is building HIS *'church'* upon
THIS revelation and nothing else.**

**Listen; there is no other knowledge, no
other foundation for us to build *'church'*
upon.**

'Church' is built and established upon
revelation knowledge, **THIS revelation
knowledge, revealed and made known in
the person of Jesus Christ,** *and no other
knowledge,* amen.

Jesus said, *"I will build My 'church,' and the
powers of death* (or the gates of hades) *shall
not prevail against it."*

Another translation says,

"...the gates of hell shall not prevail against it!"

Jesus is building HIS *'church'*!

Now, I say again, Jesus is not a building
contractor. He is not into building buildings.

And He is also not building rules and
regulations and organizations.

Jesus is building HIS *'church',* meaning He is building people. And He is building HIS *'church'* through people, living stones.

"Like living stones," Peter said, *"...we are being built together* (assembled together – knitted and welded together) *into a spiritual house* (or a house in the spirit realm), *for a dwelling place of God by the Spirit."*

Jesus is building *a people*, a holy nation, a peculiar people, a people of faith, a people of revelation knowledge, a people of insight and revelation in the knowledge of Him, a people who know His identity *and who know their true identity, as genuine children of God, revealed in Him.*

You really should get my books, *"God's Love for You!"* and *"God's Inheritance in You!"* for a greater revelation of your identity as offspring of God.

Chapter 3

The Effects of the Fall
Will Not Prevail!

And now Jesus says that this people building *will prevail over the powers of death and against the gates of hell, the gates of Hades!*

He states that this people building, this children of God building, this household of God, ***will usher into this world "My kingdom"!***

You see, **God has a purpose for His *'church'*.**

God's purpose for His *'church'* and for His revelation knowledge within His *'church'* is not survival. It is not for the *'church'* to kind of hang in there. He did not plan for just a few of them to kind of hang on until the bitter end and barely survive, until eventually it is all over and the last trumpet sounds.

No, God's purpose for His *'church'* is glorious.

God's desire for His people that He will build into this rock, into this rock revelation of Jesus, into this solid understanding of seeing themselves in Jesus, is glorious and powerful.

You see *"the powers of death"* and *"the gates of hell, the gates of Hades"* Jesus mentions in this scripture are the exact *"strongholds"*, the very *"powers of Sin and death"* Paul talks about in Romans.

Jesus and Paul both are referring to **the effects of the Fall.**

And now God says that the powers of the enemy, the **gates of hell, the gates of Hades;** *the resistance of the enemy to maintain his ground* **will not prevail against the** *'church'.*

That means that Satan may have someone in bondage to alcohol or drug addiction, or whatever destructive habits, or he may have someone else in bondage through lust and fornication and adultery and homosexuality, living an immoral life, and he has them all deceived and they are clinging to a false inferior identity of themselves, and he has all these kinds of things going on in people's lives to come and steal, kill, and destroy them (*You see, he wants to rob them of the quality of life Jesus desires for them*).

And Satan sets up his strongholds in people's lives, but Jesus says that, through this *'church'* that He is building **those strongholds will not prevail!**

That means those strongholds will be broken into by the *'church,'* and those gates of hell, those gates of hades, will be broken down and crushed, and the captives will be released by the *'church'.*

God desires to set people free through His *'church'.*   That means God desires for people to live free lives, liberated lives, lives that are set free ***through insight and understanding,*** lives that testify of the liberty that comes ***through the knowledge of Jesus.***

It is very interesting to note that the word *"**hell**"* or *"**hades**"* as used in the phrase, *"…and the gates of Hell (or Hades) shall not prevail,"* comes from a combination of the original Greek preposition, **ha,** and the Greek word, **ides,** which basically means ***not to see, or not to perceive.*** It is a word that has to do with blindness, with being blinded or with having blinders on. It is also very interesting to note that this word **ides**, is also the root word for where we get our English word **ideas** from.

You see, God desires for you and me to enjoy one quality of life only, and it is called: ***life more abundantly.***

God is not glorified through any other kind of life, which is an inferior kind of life. God cannot be glorified through a life of lack and poverty and depression and sickness and disease and whatever other *expression of darkness* you can think of.

God is glorified through a testimony of abundance!

Now that abundance is not just there magically. No, it is there as the fruit of what is plowed and what is sown.

God wants to sow into your heart and plant and establish there **the revelation of the knowledge of Jesus, so that that revelation, that insight and understanding, will become a rock, a foundation to you.**

You need a foundation to build upon. You see, you cannot afford to just build your life upon your emotions or upon some kind of argument or idea or philosophy that you've gotten a hold of somewhere. But if the revelation of Jesus comes into your heart, then God uses that revelation to lay *a rock solid foundation within* you, so that you can stand *strong* in Him and know beyond a shadow of a doubt that you will prevail against the forces of darkness.

"I will build My 'church' (My **ekklesia – those who see their true identity; who they genuinely are as children of God, as the image and likeness of God in the flesh**) *and the gates of hell* (hades) **will not prevail against them**." - Matthew 16:18

Chapter 4

I Give TO YOU the Keys

"I will build My 'church' (My **ekklesia**) *and the gates of hell* (hades) ***will not prevail against it****."*   - Matthew 16:18

And then Jesus says there in Verse 19,

"I will give you the keys of the kingdom of heaven."

In 1 John 3:8 the Bible says,

"For this purpose was the son of God made manifest: ***to destroy the works of the evil one****."*

Now we know that this scripture was making reference to Jesus, but it was also making reference to the *'church'*.

And so, even right now, the whole world is waiting ***for a manifestation of the sons of God*** *who will destroy the works of the evil one.*

You see, there must be a manifestation of this purpose, there must be a manifestation of the kingdom of God in the earth still

today, *through us, the 'church', the body of Christ, the sons and daughters of God.*

You see, while people are still thinking about it and scratching their heads and asking themselves and wondering if, *'Maybe He's a prophet?'* or *'Maybe He's Elijah?'* or *'Maybe He's John the Baptist?'*

'...You know, we're not quite sure who He is...'

'...We're not quite sure where He is,'

...as long as people are still wondering about these things, *the world will remain in the dark!*

But you see, the moment Jesus becomes manifest to anyone, *the works of the devil are destroyed.*

When you speak to someone who is in some form of bondage and you reveal the truth of Jesus to that person, *the works of darkness are destroyed.* Because you see, **when light comes in, when revelation knowledge comes in, when you are the Christ, the Son of the living God comes in, directly from God by the Holy Spirit,** *darkness flees, the blinders are taken off, and every other opinion is subdued by the truth!*

The truth of Jesus, the truth of God, TRUTH Himself conquers that other opinion.

The enemy wants to bind people's lives through sickness and disease and all kinds of addictions and other things that come to steal, kill and destroy, and hold them in captivity. *But then the truth comes to them about the revelation of Jesus,* **and people are released. *Satan's prisoners are* released,** *and "...* **the gates of hades (that spiritual blindness) cannot prevail.***"*

"I will build My 'church' and the gates of hell (hades) **will not prevail against it.***"*

"I give **to you** *the keys of the kingdom of heaven ..."* And a more accurate translation from the original Greek would read, *"Whatever you bind on earth, shall be, having been bound in heaven."*

In other words: *"...* **whatever you bind on earth, will be bound, because it is already bound in heaven.***"*

"...and whatever you loose on earth, shall be, having been loosed in heaven."

" **I give TO YOU** *the keys of the kingdom..."*

God is delegating His very own authority to His *'church'*, **to you and me as His children!** In other words, **He gives us the power of attorney.**

That word *attorney* in the dictionary means: **to be legally appointed by another in order to transact business for that person.**

God gives His *'church'*, His believers, His people, His **ekklesia,** *who know and understand their true identity as children of God restored to them in Jesus;* God gives **us** the keys of the kingdom of heaven.

The implications are huge!

It also means that God is not planning to build a church, a little building, that stands out there in a lonely field somewhere, and the people there are just doing something that is seemingly so very innocent, and *'You know, we are just kind of meeting together, sitting on our pews, having a nice little cozy comfortable time together in our little services.'*

No man, hey listen, God has entrusted this thing called *'church'*, His body, **His very own children,** with a commission: *to enforce and reinforce His integrity and His authority* **here upon earth,** *with keys; some very special and dynamic keys!*

You see, those *"gates"*, the gates of hell, (the gates of death, the gates of hades) *need to be unlocked* **because those *"gates"* hold people in prison.**

The gate is the strong place, made of metal. If you can break down the gate, the strongest place in the structure, *then those walls people put up mean nothing. It's like paper, easily broken down: it just crumbles at the sound of your voice, like the walls of Jericho!*

Chapter 5

Release the Prisoners!

Jesus has taken the keys from the enemy and He gives those keys to us in order *to release the prisoners.*

He gives those keys TO US.

Now I want you to see the implications of this. *I want us to see it clearly and accurately*

Because so often we think, *'Man, you know, God is still **going to do** a big thing in this earth, in this old world we live in, sooner or later. You know, eventually, somewhere off in the future, **He is going to** bring a massive revival, and **He is going to** release people and set them free.'*

And so we constantly pray *for that ever elusive revival* and we pray for this person and for that person and for this family member and for that one and we pray, *'Lord, **You must do something** for them and to them, **please**, because they are so blinded by darkness.'* And we pray, *'God **please do something** about this situation and about that situation'* and, *'God **please heal** aunt so-and-so and this*

47

person and that person,' and the list goes on and on, *'…God **please help** this person and that person and so-and-so, shame God, I feel sorry for them, they are so poor'* …and, *'God **please**, this'* …and, *'God **please**, that'* …and on and on we go.

But we are praying to God to do something which He's already done, *and which He has now entrusted to you and I to go and accomplish as His representatives.*

Now, of course I am not saying that I am now like a lone ranger, running out there on my own to go and accomplish these things all in my own strength. As if I don't need Jesus, as if I don't need to function out of intimate relationship with the Holy Spirit.

No! He is in me and with me and He lives through me. And as I yield to Him and listen for His direction, I do these things *as He empowers me,* and I operate *in His power,* not independent of Him, but *with* Him, *by Him, through Him.*

Jesus said, *"Without Me you can do nothing!"*

But you see that is exactly the point, ***WE ARE NOT WITHOUT HIM!***

By His Spirit He lives in us, and with us, and through us!

He said, *"Abide in Me, and I in you. As the branch cannot bear fruit of itself, unless it abides in the vine, neither can you, unless you abide in Me."*

"I am the vine, you are the branches. He who abides in Me, and I in him, bears much fruit, for without me you can do nothing!"

- John 15:4 & 5

Paul put it this way in Philippians 4:13,

*"I can do all things **through Christ who strengthens me** (who enables and empowers me)."*

Peter says something similar in Acts Chapter Three after working a miracle. First of all he said to the lame man at the gate beautiful begging for alms,

*"**Such as I have, I give unto you**: In the name of Jesus Christ of Nazareth, rise up and walk!"*

"And he took the man by the right hand and lifted him up, and immediately his feet and ankle bones received strength."

"So the man, leaping up, stood and walked and entered the temple with them – walking, leaping, and praising God."

49

Acts 3:9-12,

"And all the people saw the man walking and praising God. Then they knew that it was the same man, who sat begging alms at the Beautiful Gate of the temple, and they were filled with wonder and amazement at what had happened to him. Now as the lame man that was healed held on to Peter and John, all the people ran together to them in the porch which is called Solomon's, greatly amazed. So when Peter saw it, he responded to the people..."

Now this is what Peter said:

*"Men of Israel, **why do you marvel at this,** or why look so intently at us, **as though by our own power or godliness** we had made this man walk?"*

He continued to say in Verse 16,

"And His name (Jesus' name), *through faith in His name, has made this man strong, whom you see and know. Yes, **the faith which comes through Him** has given this man this perfect soundness in the presence of you all."*

But let me get back to the point I was making before taking this rabbit trail.

Too often we are praying to God and instead of being inspired by the faith of God, by the truth of the gospel, by the faith

of Christ within us, *by the Christ Himself who lives in us,* we end up begging God to do something <u>which He has already done</u> *and which He has now entrusted to you and I to go and accomplish as His representatives.*

Can you see how this revelation has the potential to change the mentality of the *'church'* as we know it today?

And that change is desperately needed because the modern *'church'* of today is sitting with their hands in their pockets praying for revival.

'Well, God, You better do something, because, Oh, it is such an evil time we live in today.'

And that's also why we have many now starting to pray for Heaven to come and to just come quickly, because, *'Oh God, we want to get out of this miserable old world. It's just going from bad to worse, and Oh, sin is increasing as we speak and unrighteousness is just carrying on all around us. And Oh God, we are so weak and anemic; we can't do anything at all about it.'*

No! **That's a bunch of nonsense!**

While we are carrying on in our unbelief and having our little pity parties, God is saying,

'Church, arise and shine! Wake up to the revelation which Peter received in his own heart! Wake up fully to that same revelation! You also are a child of God, and I give to <u>you</u> the keys of the kingdom!'

Chapter 6

Do Not Misunderstand Your Authority

Now before I move on, I want to add another thing in here. No one in their right mind would give the keys of their car to their little boy or girl who is only five years old. No, they are still babes!

And many today are still babes in their understanding. They will be very glad to go and play with the car, but they wouldn't know the first thing about driving that thing. And the next minute, they'll be driving it over a cliff.

Please listen very carefully to what I have to say, because you see, **God cannot entrust anyone with the keys of real revelation to His authority *before birthing in their heart and settling in their spirit a real revelation of Jesus, of His love and of His person, of who He really is,* because if that doesn't happen first, *they will end up abusing that authority!***

Just like even that same Peter did later when, at the hearing of his words, Ananias and Sapphira dropped dead at his feet in Acts 5:1-10.

That is exactly what you get from a revelation of authority without a thorough revelation or understanding of grace; of the Father and Jesus' true identity, and our true identity as children of God, which He came to restore to us in the work of redemption.

You see at that point in Peter's walk he was mixing the Law with grace, *and a little leaven leavens the whole lump. You end up focusing on sin and perpetuating the ministry of the Law and condemnation and death!*

It was the Holy Spirit Himself and the beloved apostle Paul also that had to later rescue Peter's mind and heart and help him come out from under legalism, and understand grace more thoroughly, and purge his conscience from dead works.

(Now, I know that some of you might be offended with my interpretation of the Ananias and Sapphira incident and there are pastor friends of mine that, even though they don't see this incident as God's wrath and anger and judgment, they still can somehow see it as an act of God's love, the kind of love they say, that would want to protect the rest of the assembly from the same toxic mindset of Ananias and

Sapphira, and therefore would rather kill those two people than to have their poison spread. *But in the light of redemption and reconciliation, I just cannot see it that way.*

Jesus' work of redemption has taught us that God's ultimate goal with the individual, with every single one of His kids, is reconciliation and restoration, not punishment and/or annihilation!

I also cannot quite buy the age old argument that it was almost like Uzzah who touched the ark and that the glory just got so strong upon the early *'church'* because of the great grace that was upon them, that stronger judgment than usual broke out against sin, and God's anger flared up, and He killed Ananias and Sapphira for not respecting His holy presence among them enough.

I cannot help but believe that, if that was indeed the case, then a whole lot more people would still be dropping like flies all over the place today.

I say again: *To me, this viewpoint is diametrically opposed to the nature of the God who is love! It totally goes against redemption realities. It completely goes against the Father's heart for restoration and reconciliation. It just does not line up with our Daddy's love for each and every one of His children.*)

Listen, there is nothing in love that wants to kill and destroy. God is pure love personified. Therefore there is nothing in God that wants to kill and destroy!

Everything in God, everything in LOVE, wants to redeem and restore and rescue people out of deception, even out of self-deception, instead of judging them, condemning them, and destroying them.

Jesus revealed a God who would rather be judged and condemned and face hell himself than to judge and condemn us.

He revealed a Father that would rather take our judgment upon Himself, and be judged in our place, rather than see us judged.

If we have seen Jesus, *then we have seen the Father.*

Jesus said, *"I did not come into the world to condemn the world, but that the world through Me might be saved!"*   - John 3:17

He also said this in John 12:47,

"If anyone hears My words and does not believe them, I do not judge him; for I did not come to judge the world, but to save the world."

A legalistic Law mentality will turn you into a vigilante if you don't watch it. Like the sons of thunder in Luke 9:52-55 who wanted to call down fire from heaven, to consume the ones who resisted them and weren't receiving Jesus' ministry, just like they remembered Elijah doing in 2 Kings 1:10. But Jesus rebuked the disciples for thinking that way, and said to them,

"You don't know what spirit you're of..."

If they really knew the Spirit of God, and what He is really like, if they really knew the God who is love, if they really knew His nature, if they really knew what spirit they were of, if they really knew what the image and likeness of God looks like, what the Divine nature looks like that they are partakers of and that is within them, they would not be acting that way!

In order to be entrusted with the keys to God's authority, it is absolutely vital that we first get a real revelation of Jesus and who He really is, birthed in our hearts!

We have to have it settled in our spirits that He is the God of compassion.

He is love. And we must know Him that way, amen!

We must know Him as LOVE before we can flow with His Spirit and properly operate in His authority!

Paul said in 2 Corinthians 10:8 and 13:10 that the Lord gave us authority **for building up, *not for tearing down.***

It is impossible for the *'church'* of Jesus Christ to conquer and to walk in authority properly *without an accurate understanding of the revelation of Jesus Christ.*

Chapter 7

Having Been Loosed Already

Within the revelation of Jesus Christ, God gives us a key, so that, with that key of His redemption truth, and of His love, we may release the prisoners; *we may unlock their minds and hearts and set them free!*

We may unlock what is reality; we may unlock reality to them, we may unlock what is *"...having been loosed in heaven."*

People are loosed in heaven! They are already loosed in heaven! They have already been loosed in that unseen realm of spirit reality!

God determined in heaven that He would liberate and redeem Man and He did just that in Christ, in that work of redemption, through the shed blood of Jesus.

So in heaven, in that unseen realm of reality, in the spirit realm of reality, God has already released all mankind.

Paul says in 2 Corinthians 5:15 that, *"From now on we can no longer judge any man from a human point of view* (from a natural reality only)."

Why Paul?

Because (Verse 14), *"For Christ's love compels us!"*

"Because we are convinced that one died for all," he says, *"and therefore all died."*

Paul wants us to grasp and understand that a death has already occurred; *Man is already redeemed.*

Man is already released. He is already healed.

*"By His stripes we **were** healed!"* (Past tense)

Now Jesus says, *"**I give <u>unto you</u> the keys** of the kingdom of heaven…"*

*"…**so that you can now go and unlock what is already unlocked in heaven**…"*

*"…**and so that you can now go and bind what is already bound in heaven**."*

Satan doesn't have any room to operate in heaven! He doesn't have any say in heaven! He doesn't have any basis left to operate from!

God is not sitting there in heaven with a headache, you know, because He's got so many problems because Satan is giving Him trouble all the time.

No man, listen, **God has restricted the enemy's freedom of movement to zero in heaven. There is no room for the enemy to operate in heaven.**

And now Jesus says to us, His *'church'*,

*"I give **to you** the keys of the kingdom of heaven **so that there on earth you can put a stop to the enemy's activity and actions round about you!"***

As the *'church'* **we really must receive this as truth, as reality, NOW!**

Redemption happened, amen, and redemption was a success, amen.

If we really get a hold of this revelation *and become fully persuaded in it **and make it our own,*** it will change our attitude towards **what we can and cannot do.**

And then the fullness of the love and faith of Christ inside of us will finally be able to find unrestricted flow, unrestricted expression.

In this revelation realized and embraced, the days of pew sitting, of mere pew warming are over, *because we will be using these keys Jesus gave us to put a stop and an end to Satan's activity in our own lives.*

There is no use in trying to go and liberate someone else *if there is still a log in your own eye.* **You can't really set anyone free if you are still walking in immorality and in this, that, and the next thing, and you are still bound by sin,** *and accommodating the works of the evil one.*

"For this purpose was the Son of God made manifest: **To destroy the works of the evil one!***"*   - 1John 3:8

God wants to utterly destroy the works of the evil one! That means He wants to paralyze his authority: *the lies, the deception of darkness* **that keep your life in bondage.**

God knows that once He has established that truth of His, concerning a successful redemption, in your heart, then He'll also be able, through you, to release your neighbor who is still in bondage, as well as the next person, and the next person, and so on, and so on, and so on.

Let's look at Psalm 115:16.

"The heavens are the Lord's heavens…"

62

That means you and I can't do anything about changing heaven, amen.

"…but the earth He has given to the sons of Men."

God has given us the land! He has given us the earth! He has given us the nations as our inheritance, the very ends of the earth as our possession!

He said to natural Israel, *"Possess the land!"*

"Oh God, but there's giants out there, haven't You seen them God?!"

"Go in this thy might Gideon!"

Kaleb and Joshua had a different spirit. *"We are well able to overcome! Because the Lord is for us!"*

"…and if God is for us, who can be against us?!"

Listen, *"The earth He has given to the sons of Men!"*

"I give to YOU the keys of the kingdom!"

"I will build MY 'church'…"

I see the building of Jesus' *'church'* as the building up of a people, through redemption

truth, who are therefore prepared in their spirits, and equipped in their inner-man, to go with that same truth and conquer the works of darkness, and release its prisoners, and take its spoil, in the power and enablement of the Holy Spirit.

That's what God sees for His *'church'*.

Chapter 8

Church
Through the Eyes of God

We need to start looking at the *'church'* through the eyes of God!

We can ask ten different people, *"What do you think the 'church' is?"* And we'll have ten different answers. We'll have ten different traditions perhaps, or ten different denominations represented, and ten different opinions.

But listen to me now: it doesn't matter who says what, it doesn't even matter what the Pope says about the *'church'*. **What matters is what the eternal, living Word of God says about His *'church'*.**

It only matters what God says about <u>His</u> *'church'*.

The only definition of *'church'* that matters is the definition God has already given in the Scriptures concerning that word *'church'*.

If Jesus is building His *'church',* surely He has an exact plan in mind for what it should look like.

God works all things according to the purpose of His will.

He does not just start building something without having a blueprint, without having an exact design in mind.

He doesn't just start by putting a little brick here and there and stand back looking at it and think, *'Well, that looks nice, I think I'll go with that.'*

He doesn't work like that. He doesn't just put bricks down at random and then embrace it as His plan. No man, that thing would be a mess; it would eventually turn out to be nothing but a concoction!

God knows what He is after, when it comes to His *'church'.* God is a God of destiny! He is a God of intent and purpose!

Did you know that God has a very specific intent and purpose and call upon your life?

You are called into the fellowship of the Son.

You are called into the fullness of the measure of the stature of Christ.

You are called to be the very expression of the image and likeness of the invisible God.

You are called to be His witness, to be the very nature of God on display.

You are called to spread that fragrance wherever you go. You are called to be the aroma of Christ upon the earth. You are called to be the salt and the light of the world.

You are called to be the body of Christ.

The Spirit of God within you cries out: Abba Father; Daddy God!

As God's very own child you are called to be God's representative, God's ambassador.

You are called to represent His authority and dominion upon the earth.

You are called to be sons of light, putting darkness to flight everywhere you go!

The Bible says that you are a living stone. That means God has a place for you to fit into this building. You are an exact fit, to fit into this building, into this vehicle called the 'church'.

You are an exact fit, to fit into this plan of God that He wants to release through that vehicle of His *'church', through His children, through you,* to conquer the darkness and take back the earth from the evil one.

Listen, God is not just going to wipe out the earth and say, *"Well, you know, this thing was a colossal failure, so I am just going to give up on this lot and start over."*

No! God has made an eternal investment into this earth, and at the same time, *He has also made an eternal investment in your life! You truly are His child, and nothing is going to change that!*

You are of immense value and worth to Him, in fellowship, yes, and also then as part of His strategy for His *'church'* to win back this planet, to win back His lost and confused, kidnapped kids.

So God wants to love you and fellowship with you, and equip you, in order to release you, so that you then can also be able to go and release the prisoners of darkness, the ones taken captive by Satan. They don't belong to him, they are Gods children; Gods kidnapped kids.

Okay, now turn with me, if you have your Bible handy, to Ephesians Chapter Three.

If you don't have a Bible at hand, it's okay, you can go and study it later, just keep reading for now.

I want us to see this building Jesus was talking about when He said, *"I will build My 'church' and the gates of hell, the gates of hades, shall not prevail against it."*

I thank God that it's not a comfortable nice little old rock building, and there is saint Peter, standing at the door, with the key in his hand, you know, and his only job is to open the door on a Sunday morning for church, and to close it again after the church service, and he repeats it again on Wednesday nights, and so it goes on week after week.

That, my brethren has been our concept of *'church'* **for way too long.** It's been our Sunday school concept *for long enough!*

I am here to tell you that we must get rid of such a concept, *because it's the wrong concept!* It is not God's concept of the *'church'* and of *'the keys of the kingdom'*!

We have had an elementary Sunday school mentality about *'church'* and about *'the keys of the kingdom'* for way too long!

And we call our little *'church'* Saint Peter's, and we pride ourselves that our *'church'* is built on Saint Peter, or Saint Rudi, or Saint whatever.

69

And we can just add and build on Saint Peter and His teaching, or Saint Moses and his teaching, or Saint so-and-so, and so on, and so forth.

But let me tell you, *God wants to build <u>His</u> 'church',* not ours, or this denomination's *'church,'* or that denomination's *'church'* but, *"I will build <u>MY</u> 'church.'"*

And let me say again, Jesus is not a building contractor up in heaven. He is not building mansions in the sky. No!

He has gone and prepared a place for us, through His death on the cross, and through His resurrection, a place of being seated with Him in heaven, *in a place of authority.* He has gone to prepare a place for us of ruling and reigning with Him, *through His work of redemption.*

He has prepared that place for you and for me as children of God, so that we may be where He is, one with Him and seated with Him in the bosom of our Father, of our Daddy, ruling and reigning with Him.

And now He is saying to us, *"As I am, even so are you!"*

"As the Father has sent me, so send I you!"

Chapter 9

*Brought Near
by the Blood of Christ*

But before I get carried away, let's get to
Ephesians Chapter Three. I want us to take a
look at this building whose builder and maker is
God. Well, we'll get to Ephesians Chapter
Three, but let's first go to Ephesians 2:12,

*"Now remember that you were at one time
separated from Christ..."*

Is that hard to remember?

Listen, I dare say, most of us have all come to
realize that there was a time when we just
didn't have anything going for us.

I mean, Christ, at one point was totally
unattractive to us; *we couldn't care less about
Him.* We couldn't care less about God, or
about the future or about death, or about
anything spiritual, or about *'church'.*

We just cared about our own future needs, and
about our own immediate needs that had to get
met right now.

The only time we prayed was: *"God I want patience and I want it now!"*

Ha… ha… ha… Let's face it, we only prayed when we really had a need, and we thought, *"Well let's cry out to this God everyone is talking about, this unknown moody old God, maybe He can help."*

But that was our whole religious life,

And some of you might still be there today.

Ha… ha… ha…

But we were without Christ, we were ignorant, we were walking and stumbling about in darkness. And *'church'* to us was only something with a high tower or a pinnacle or a something, with a bell or a cockroach nest and some bird poop or something up there… ha… ha… ha…

It might as well have been for all we could imagine, amen.

Don't laugh now okay, because you know, that was our whole concept of the thing. And God was some miserable old being somewhere up in the sky somewhere, who was sitting out there staring down on us with a disapproving gaze, just ready to zap us when we were naughty and stepped out of line.

So we stayed right out of His way. We wanted to get as far away as possible from this moody old God, because there was nothing attractive about Him.

You see the father of lies had us kidnapped and bound up in deception.

And that father of lies would seek to steel, and destroy and to kill and to take love away from us and keep God away from us.

The devil doesn't mind you having a nice time for a while, but while the candy-floss is still sweet in your mouth, he puts poison in your stomach.

So here in Ephesians 2:12 God says,

"...at one time you were separated from Christ."

You see, before I can fully discover who I am in Christ, I usually have to realize who I was without Him. I was separated from Him, a nobody, going nowhere! Really, that is the truth!

Even with all my prominence and with all my talents and my dignity, I was still just a nobody, going nowhere fast!

Oh I could have a fat bank account, with the nicest car in town, or the most beautiful hotty at my side, or whatever. But still I was a nobody going nowhere, because we all bleed alike and we die alike! From dust we came and to dust we just go, and that's it, that was my destiny.

My destiny was as good as dust...*without Christ.*

They could bury me in a pine coffin or just a cardboard box, or even a gold, silver, or chrome plated Mahogany casket, it doesn't matter you know. The thing just rots after a while, you know, it's just dust. And what's the value of dust? Next to nothing, amen!

"...at one time you were separated from Christ."

"Alienated from the commonwealth of Israel. Strangers to the covenants of promise..."

Amen, that's true!

Covenant wasn't even in our vocabulary.

What's promise?

I don't even know what that means!

All I remember and know about is that at one point somebody promised me something and never kept their promise. And likewise, I promised many things to various people, and I never kept mine either. So what is *"promise,"* and what is *"covenant?"*

But suddenly, now that I am reconciled to Jesus, now that I have discovered the seed of His Word and of His Spirit that has been given birth to in my heart through the revelation of Jesus, the revelation that He is love, that He is the Christ, the Son of the living God, suddenly, through that revelation that He loves me, I have been set free, and made whole!

I have discovered that He is not just some religious fanatic. No, He is the very Christ, the Son of the living God, and He is *'yeshua hamashiach.'* **He is my savior, and he loves me!** He is Jesus who has come to redeem me and release me from my sin and from all the power of darkness and from Satan himself!

And if I've seen Him, I've seen Love Himself; I've seen the Father who loves me!

And if I've seen Jesus, I've also seen myself, my true self, my original self, my authentic, original design I was designed for, as child of God, as the image and likeness of God, there on display in Him. That exact design I was redeemed for, to give expression to, and which I also was released into, as the truth of the gospel dawned on me.

I have discovered that, in Jesus I have been made a partaker in that eternal, unbreakable blood covenant!

I am not just drifting around in this inferior, insignificant little, casual, relationship with a confusing God I do not really know.

No, but I have a strong, eternal, unbreakable covenant with God Almighty, *with God my true Father, my Daddy, **who loves me!***

I have a legal relationship to every promise through Jesus Christ!

That means that every promise in this New Testament, in the gospel and in the New Testament scriptures, every promise which concerns Man, *is meant for me.* **It's my inheritance, amen!**

And you see that has changed my attitude towards the Word, it has changed my attitude towards the promises.

Notice what Paul says here in Ephesians 2:13-15,

"But now in Christ Jesus, you who once were far off have been brought near in the blood of Christ. For He is our peace, who has made us both one, and broken down the wall of hostility, by abolishing in His flesh, the Law of commandments, so making peace."

Chapter 10

God's Dwelling Place

Ephesians 2:19 says,

*"So then you are no longer strangers and foreigners, but you are fellow citizens with the saints and **members of the household of God**."*

He is referring to that building whose builder and maker is God. You are the *'church'*. Not some building, no, you are the *'church'*,

*"...**members of the household of God**."*

You are the *'church'*, and the *'church'* is the household of God! Can you begin to see what this building looks like?!

God is giving us a clear picture of the *'church'* He has in mind. He is giving us a clear picture of **HIS** *'church'*.

He says, *"Remember, you guys, you were at one time outside, **but now you are inside**..."*

Not inside a building, *but inside **a household!***

Don't stare at the building you are meeting in and think, *"Well, this thing doesn't even look like a 'church'."*

Listen, no building is supposed to look like the *'church'.* It cannot even come close to looking like the *'church'.* It's just supposed to be a shell or a shelter that keeps the sun and the rain out while **the *'church'* family** is gathering and meeting together.

You are the *'church',* amen!

People are God's building! And God wants to build something into their lives, *into your life,* amen!

God wants to build a capacity into your life to accommodate the fullness of His presence! He wants your life to become *His sanctuary,* amen! That is what *'church'* is all about!

Can you now see why God despises sin, why He despises darkness?! Because darkness, and its fruit of sin, would spoil His sanctuary. *It ruins you!* '

It ruins your enjoyment of His presence! It ruins your sense of oneness with God!

Walking in darkness and entertaining sin in your life, deliberately entertaining darkness in your life, is like saying to God, *"God, You are no longer welcome in my life! I would much rather treasure these nice little vibes and things I get from my sin, from my idol, that make me feel so good for a while. I would much rather accommodate darkness, I would much rather accommodate Satan in my life than You, God!"*

But Jesus says, "I have come to set the captives free!"

And so all the while the Holy Spirit is still standing there, the Father is still standing there, Jesus is still standing there, and they are saying,

"We will never let you go! We love you more than you know! We will not give up on you! We will keep trying to reach you! We will keep at it! Our love is relentless! We will keep on loving you until we get the breakthrough, until we break through to your heart, until we wear down the enemy's stronghold within your thinking, until we wear down your stubborn resistance and your ignorance and that deception you are in!"

Notice what God is saying and what He is trying to get us to see here in Ephesians 2:19,

*"**You are no longer strangers and foreigners, but fellow citizens with the saints and members of the household of God!**"*

Isn't that just beautiful?! Oh how much He loves us!

Let's take a look at this building, the *'church'*. Let's take a look at this household. *Look at how God establishes it and strengthens it.*

The first thing you do with a building is dig a foundation *so deep* and you make it *so thoroughly strong* that it can handle pressure.

So, let's look at this household, this building. Look at its foundation with me. The first thing you do is you establish a foundation.

Ephesians 2:20,

"Built upon the foundation of the apostles and the prophets…"

The prophetic bits and pieces of times gone by, the prophetic foresight of the Old Testament prophets became part of the foundation, part of the very rock solid insight and revelation of the apostles for this building, for this *'church,'* for this household of God to live in and live by.

"Built upon the foundation of the apostles and the prophets…"

Those are the guys sent forth with the Word, *still today they are being sent forth, amen,* **because how can you believe until you've heard?**

You used to just believe what your think-tank told you, *but then you heard the Word, the truth of the gospel.*

And now suddenly the Word of God came to you through those sent to you to deliver the Word, and it challenged your thinking *and you changed your mind and believed the gospel.*

"You are no longer strangers and foreigners, but fellow citizens with the saints and members of the household of God!"

"Built upon the foundation of the apostles and the prophets, with Christ Jesus Himself being the chief cornerstone…"

Not Peter? No, Christ Jesus Himself!

"…with Christ Jesus Himself being the chief cornerstone, in whom the whole structure is joined together (knitted together, welded together, or cemented together, by the abiding Christ, by the abiding Spirit of Christ, and through the abiding Word, through the abiding truth of redemption.)…"

"*In Him* (in Christ) *the whole structure is joined together and grows into a holy temple in the Lord.*"

Now Verse 22 reemphasizes it and makes it personal, just in case we may overlook it, or argue against such a concept.

It sounds to me like God *really* wants us to get the revelation, He wants you and I to grasp this fully that,

"In Him **YOU ALSO** *are being built together, or assembled together, and assimilated into this building, into the 'church',* **as part of this family, as members of this household, for a dwelling place of God in the spirit***."*

The gospel, the love of God on display in redemption, God's love for you, is the very cement that holds the *'church'* together.

His love for us, revealed to us, is what knits and joins our hearts together with His, *and with one another.*

His love knits us to Christ, *and to one another,* to accommodate the very presence of God, both individually and corporately as a body of believers, as the body of Christ.

God's design, God's purpose for His *'church',* His household, for the members of that household, for you and for me, is to accommodate the very presence of God; *to be a dwelling place of God in the spirit!*

Let this sink into your heart: God wants your life to be a dwelling place for Him in the spirit. God wants to come and dwell in your life!

We are studying what God has in mind for His *'church,'* what He wants it to look like, amen.

Chapter 11

Manifesting God's Power

Let's jump over to Ephesians Chapter Three real quickly, and let's take a look at what He further has to say about what He is building.

He goes on and He says in Verse 10 of Ephesians 3,

"God's desire for the 'church' (for us, for you and for me as children of God) is **to manifest the manifold wisdom of God** (in other words, **what God accomplished in Christ in that work of redemption on humanities behalf**);"

"God's desire for the 'church' (for us, for you and for me as children of God) is to manifest **all of that**, *referred to as the manifold superior wisdom of God,* **to the principalities and the powers in heavenly places***..."*

God wants to show the forces of darkness that they can no longer rule where He has established His reign.

He wants to show that to them, **through His 'church',** not through a building, or a program, or an organization, *but through people, through* individuals, **through you and I who understand our true identity as children of God.**

God wants to show these things to the principalities and powers and the forces of darkness, **through a people of faith, a people who actually walk in the liberty that He came to give to us through the blood of Jesus.**

Paul goes on to say in Ephesians 3:11 that,

"This was according to the eternal purpose which He has realized in Christ Jesus our Lord."

God realized His eternal purpose; *He revealed it in Christ Jesus.* **His eternal purpose in Christ Jesus *was unveiled*, and then He also *realized it* in Christ Jesus. He made it reality!**

God's eternal purpose was for mankind, for you and me to comprehend and walk in our true identity as children of God.

Ephesians 3:14 & 15 then says,

*"**For this reason** I bow my knees before the Father, from whom every family in heaven and on earth is named…"*

For what reason?

86

For the reason of God's eternal purpose having been made reality. For the reason of mankind's release. For the reason of God desiring to manifest that release. For the reason of God manifesting His power. God wants to manifest that power *through us, the 'church'*, <u>*through you and through me*</u>.

Paul says, *'Now listen, I realize that God wants to build a 'church', a strong building, a stronghold, out of people. God wants to build for Himself a dwelling place out of people. But God's people that He embraces and uses to build this stronghold out of, are not people who are strong and wealthy and beautiful on the outside, in the flesh. They are that in the spirit.*

*God wants to build people up in the spirit to look like that, to be beautiful and wealthy and strong in the spirit. God wants to build people up in faith and in the spirit **to be strong in the power of His might.***'

See, this thing is not made out of flesh and blood. It's not carnal; it's not a natural thing. It is spirit, it's a spiritual thing, we are talking spirit dimension here, spirit identity!

*...**A dwelling place of God in the spirit.***

You know, we think that if we want to get a good *'church'* going, we need to get a couple of influential guys involved, and wealthy people, and a bunch of talented folk, and we'll simply put all that natural talent and resources together and we'll have a good *'church'* going.

Listen, God's not looking at this thing called *'church'* from Man's point of view.

God is only focused on His eternal purpose accomplished in Christ Jesus.

That intention, that purpose was to redeem mankind, to reconcile His lost and confused, kidnapped kids back unto Himself! And that then is what He has accomplished in Christ Jesus!

And now God's only focus is on that eternal purpose!

In the light of that eternal purpose revealed and accomplished in Christ Jesus, God is not looking at anything concerning His *'church'* from a mere natural standpoint, from a human point of view.

God is only looking at that eternal intention and that eternal purpose *being made known to all mankind in order for it to come into its full fruition.*

That is what God is focused upon now.

That is what God is focusing all His energy and all His power upon.

I say again, God is not looking at this from man's point of view.

God is only looking at His eternal purpose, which is to redeem mankind, which He already did over 2,014 years ago now. In heaven it's a reality!

But He now wants a people whom He can entrust with His keys of revelation and power, to go and set Mankind free and enforce what is already loosed and bound in heaven.

That means we who hear these things, and perhaps see and understand and grasp them, can no longer afford to sit around with our hands in our pockets and shake our heads as if we don't know what to do. *For we already know what to do.*

We already know what we can and cannot do. We already know what we are allowed to do by God Himself!

We can resist the devil ourselves in our own lives, until we put the enemy to flight. And we can put the works of the evil one to a stop in other people's lives.

We can put Satan to flight if we would only believe it and embrace it as an already established reality!

Our fear and our unbelief is the only thing holding us back from living in victory ourselves, and from setting the captives free!

We used to be so blind that we thought that if we wanted to resist the devil we would have to pray, *'Oh God, please resist the devil, please get him off our backs, God!'*

But listen, there is enough truth revealed now in the work of redemption to where we understand that God is not going to resist the devil for us. He already overcame him. He's got no business with the devil anymore.

Listen, the devil is now your business and my business!

God says, *"You resist the devil ...and he will flee from YOU!"*

"You resist him steadfast in the faith!"

"...he will flee from YOU!"

"I give to YOU the keys of the kingdom"

Amen!

Hallelujah!

So, can you now see where and how we have wasted our time praying, *'God, please move. God, please do something.'*

No, listen: **YOU do it!**

Because He has already placed in your hand the key, the revelation of His lordship over death and hell, and His lordship over sickness and disease, and His lordship over poverty and lack.

And He has revealed to us that we are truly God's children and that we reign with Him and that we can now live the abundant life that He desires for us to live!

So, *"**For this reason** I bow my knees before the Father, from whom every family in heaven and on earth is named..."* (Ephesians 3:14 & 15)

Now look, Paul is writing this letter to a bunch of Christian fanatics, a bunch of faith fanatics like us. They are awakened in the spirit, they know they are born from above, they truly know they are children of God, and they are growing in grace. That means their understanding and comprehension of redemption realities is growing and so they are becoming more and more persuaded in these things, and so their love and faith is growing, and they are doing fine.

But now Paul writes to them and he says to them, *'Now listen people, God wants to build a structure, a stronghold, a temple, a dwelling place within you, so that you can become His vehicle here upon the earth. The heavens are the Lords, but the earth He has given to the sons of Men.'* He says, *'…and to this end, I am now praying for you.'*

What exactly are you praying Paul?

Are you praying that heaven will come quickly and we can all get out of this mess because it is such a miserable old world, full of heartache and sorrows, troubles and problems?

No! Thank God, no!

*"I pray that the eyes of your understanding will be enlightened, that you might intimately and fully know what the riches of the glory of His inheritance **in YOU** are!"*

"And that you may also fully know and understand what is the exceeding greatness of His power towards you who believe!"

"That power is according to His great and mighty power that He worked in Christ in reversing the fall."

"It is according to that resurrection power that He worked in Christ when He raised Him from the dead, and by which He also raised you up

with Him, and by which He made you to sit with Christ in heavenly places, in the bosom of the Father, and at the very right hand of the Father, in a place of authority, far above every principality, and every other power and might and dominion, and every name that can possibly be named as an enemy."

*"**For this reason** I bow my knees before the Father, from whom every family in heaven and on earth is named…"*

I want you to see that **God has a legal claim upon every family in heaven and upon the earth!**

Listen, God has a legal claim even upon that stubborn old neighbor or family member of yours.

When God places His name upon something that means He claims it as His.

Why did God do this?

Because you see, God is the Creator. **He legally created us and He legally redeemed us.** He has a right to, amen. He is the only One who has a right to claim it all, amen. So, He can have us, legally, amen. The devil can't have us, amen, legally or otherwise, because he is merely the father of lies. He is not the father of anything. He has created nothing.

Not a thing, amen. So, God can legally have us, amen, and the devil can't, amen.

It may be a fact that the devil has built walls around people's minds through different arguments and ideas, and given them plenty of excuses and reasons why they shouldn't and wouldn't believe in Jesus. *But listen, **you have the keys to release them!***

In the revelation of redemption, in the revelation of our authentic original sonship restored to us, in the revelation of Jesus Christ, you have the keys to unlock those prison bars of bronze and to break into that stronghold and open that gate to set that person free on the inside.

You have all the keys necessary to liberate that child of God and take the enemy's spoil from him.

You are the light of the world.

You are the salt of the earth.

I used to think that *only* Jesus could be the salt of the earth, that *only* Jesus could be the light of the world. And He IS the salt of the earth and the light of the world, **but He has said for us to be also,** amen. Because He has gone back to Heaven, and right now He is in that unseen heavenly realm, in those unseen heavenly places, and He wants to shine forth out of that unseen realm of spirit reality, *through your life,* by His Spirit, **who IS in <u>you</u> and LIVES in <u>you</u>,** amen!

Jesus wants to influence your environment *through you,* amen. *He wants **YOU** to influence your environment.* He doesn't want you to be influenced by your environment!

Ephesians 3:14- 21,

*"**For this reason** I bow my knees before the Father, from whom every family in heaven and on earth is named…"*

"…So that, according to the riches of His glory, He may grant you to be strengthened with might (with ability, with enablement, **with power**) *through His Spirit, in the inner-man."*

God wants to make *your spirit* **strong!**

And so Paul therefore prays *that God would make your inner-man, your spirit,* **strong!**

How, and why?

*"…**that Christ may dwell in your heart through faith**,"*

God wants Christ to dwell in your heart and be manifested in all His glory and power in your life, <u>through faith</u>!

Christ dwells in our hearts <u>through faith</u>, *by our seeing and comprehending and embracing fully the truth of the gospel, amen!*

Christ also manifests Himself in all His glory and power through your life, *through the same faith, amen!*

It's all through faith, amen! It's all through God's faith that comes to us (Romans 10:17). **Faith gets imparted to us by the Spirit of God as we comprehend and believe the gospel!**

It's the love of God realized that activates that faith! (Galatians 5:6).

But let's get back to Ephesians 3:17-21,

"...that Christ may dwell in your heart <u>through faith</u>,"

*"...that you, **being rooted and grounded in love**, may have power to comprehend, with all the saints..."*

Not to walk in darkness with all the saints. No, *but to walk in the light of the revelation of the knowledge of God!*

"...may comprehend together with all the saints, what is the breath, and the length, and

96

*the height, and the depth **of the love of God**..."*

That means **to intimately know the full impact of the power of that love, the full impact of the power of the living God, *the full impact of the power of <u>Christ within me</u>,* amen!**

*"...**to know the love of Christ** which surpasses mere knowledge..."*

*"...**that you may be filled with all the fullness of God!**"*

*"Now to Him who, **by the power at work within us,** is able to do far more abundantly, than all that we have the nerve to ask or think, yes, to Him be glory in the 'church' and in Christ Jesus, **throughout all generations, and to impact all generations, for ever and ever.** Amen."*

In Ephesians 6:10 Paul says,

*"Finally brethren, be strong in the Lord **and in the power of His might** (in the power of His ability and enablement)..."*

Listen, God wants to exhibit and manifest His ability and His power which He has deposited *within your spirit!*

Chapter 12

The Church In Action

I want us to go and take a look at Acts Chapter Two. I just quickly want to show you this *'church'* of the Lord Jesus Christ *in action.*

Here is the same man, Peter, and he is preaching almost the whole of Chapter Two and he is preaching with great boldness and great anointing, and in Acts 2:37 we see the response of his audience.

"When they heard this they were cut to the heart…"

The sharp contrast of the truth they were hearing to what they had previously believed about Jesus cut them to the heart. A circumcision was taking place in their minds and in their hearts.

"…they were cut to the heart."

"When they heard this…" When they heard what Peter said, they didn't keep sitting there or standing there with their own opinions. They didn't hold on to their own opinions, they didn't hold on to their own arguments and

contradictions and their own feelings and their own ideas about the matter. No a circumcision took place; *"…they were cut to the heart!"*

That means what came out of Peter's mouth was so profound that it *had an impact upon their hearts, it convinced their hearts!*

"…they were cut to the heart!"

And they yielded to what was happening, they didn't resist it, they yielded to what the Holy Spirit, the Spirit of Truth was doing in them.

And so they said to Peter and the rest of the apostles, *"Brethren, what shall we do?"*

Peter said, *"Repent and be immersed, every one of you, into the name of Jesus Christ…"*

That means be identified with Him, with His reputation and accomplishment on that cross, identify yourselves with Him,

"…in the forgiveness of sins; and you shall receive the gift of the Holy Spirit (the indwelling of the Holy Spirit.)."

Verse 39 says,

"For the promise is to you and to your children and to all those who are far off… Save yourselves from this crooked generation." So they did just that.

Acts 2:41 says,

"Not all of them, but some of them received (or embraced) *Peter's word and were immersed* (into the name of Jesus Christ, which means they embraced His reputation and His accomplishment on that cross on their behalf and thus they fully identified themselves with Him personally and embraced Him)..."

"...and there were added to the 'church' that day about three thousand souls."

Verse 42 says,

"And they devoted themselves to the apostles' teaching and fellowship, to the breaking of bread (eating together) *and to prayer* (intimate fellowship and conversation with God)."

"And fear (a passionate, reverential awe and respect and love for God) *came upon all of them. And many signs and wonders were done through the apostles."*

"And all who believed were together (they were knitted together in their hearts with such a spirit of unity, and such love for one another,) *they had all things in common, and* (they were so filled with the love of God, with love for one another, that) *they sold their possessions and goods and distributed them to all, as any had need."*

Acts 2:46 & 47 says,

"And day by day, they together attended the temple, and broke bread (had meals) *together in their homes, and they ate their food with glad and generous hearts, praising God and having favor with all the people. And the Lord added to their number day by day those who were being saved."*

Where did Peter get this ability from to persuade these hardened Jews, steeped in their religious traditions?

I mean they were so set in their ways, steeped for years and years and years in the customs and traditions and beliefs of their fathers. And now suddenly this young man, named Peter, who was a fisherman by trade, and didn't have much going for him, no academic qualifications whatsoever, began to preach to them.

This young man, Peter, was standing before this big crowd, representatives from just about every nation of the known world at the time, and he now began to boldly preach without any fear, without any intimidation.

And he just boldly proclaimed the resurrection, and the power of God, and the fact that in Jesus all of mankind was represented, and that Jesus died for man's sins.

But where did He get this ability from? And where did he get all this from? Where did he get it all from?

It was because, remember, he was in that crowd in Luke Chapter 24, when Jesus unfolded to their understanding the Scriptures, and Peter's heart also had that witness that Jesus is indeed the Christ.

And with that revelation of what all the Christ embodies and represents, the undoing of the fall and the restoration of Mankind to their original design and sonship, the foundation was laid for the *'church'.*

It is the revelation that Jesus is the Christ, the Son of the living God, that revelation of what He represents in His person and what He actually came to accomplish that *cuts through the hearts.*

Chapter 13

Supernatural Power

Besides the revelation of the identity of Jesus and the truth of redemption, I see another ingredient in the revelation of Jesus and in this New Covenant *'church'* that was present in their ministry. That is *the evidence of the supernatural.*

And not just the element of it noticeable in revelation impartation, *but the element of power for healings and miracles and signs and wonders.*

Look with me and let's read again in that same chapter of Acts.

Acts 2:22,

"Men of Israel, hear these words; Jesus of Nazareth, a man attested to you by God, with mighty works and wonders and signs, which God did through Him, in your very midst, as you yourselves know"

Peter basically said, *'I want to draw your attention to the ministry of this man, Jesus, whom you crucified. His ministry was*

accompanied by mighty signs and wonders.
God did all this through Him!'

Notice also there in the same chapter, we've
already read, but let's read it again.

Acts 2:43,

"And fear (a passionate, reverential awe and
respect and love for God) *came upon all of*
*them, **and many signs and wonders were***
***done through the apostles**."*

I want you to see in both these Scriptures I just
quoted that **God's power works**
supernaturally through ordinary men.

God manifested His power supernaturally,
and He did it through regular, everyday
people; ordinary men.

So, the evidence of the supernatural was a
sure ingredient in the life and ministry of Jesus
and in the life and ministry of the *'church'*.

They were operating in that power just like
Jesus did, and like Jesus said they would.

Jesus said in John 14:12 that the same
works He did we shall do also, and greater,
because of His work of redemption, and
because of the indwelling Holy Spirit in us.

The *'church'* was operating in that power.

106

They were not just sitting there and absorbing and enjoying the revelation of Jesus, and *'Oh, it's so wonderful God that You've blessed us with this wonderful revelation of Jesus and His work of redemption, and we are just going to sit here and enter into Your rest, and sit here in our buildings and just praise You and love on You all day…'*

No, they started going out with that revelation and with that supernatural Holy Spirit and His power residing in them. And they went and started being led by the Spirit in operating that power and they started seeing results. They started getting the prisoners of darkness released, amen! They started setting the captives free who were bound by all kinds of works of darkness, amen!

They started doing exactly what Jesus did.

In Acts 10:38, Peter made clear exactly what Jesus did as a man, how He demonstrated the supernatural power of God in His earthly ministry,

"…God anointed Jesus of Nazareth with the Holy Spirit's power; He went about doing good, healing all that were oppressed by the devil, for God was with Him."

They also started doing exactly what Jesus did *and what He told them they could do, and basically instructed them to go and do in His name.*

We read about it there in the add-on at the end of the book of Mark.

Somebody, one of the later church fathers perhaps, felt it an important enough of an issue to add it there to the end of the book of Mark. It basically reads:

Mark 16:15-18,

"And He said to them, 'Go into the entire world and preach the gospel to everyone. He who believes gets immersed and made whole; but he who does not believe continues in condemnation. And these signs will follow those who believe; In My Name they will cast out demons; they will speak with new tongues; they will by accident take up serpents and perhaps even drink poison, but nothing shall by any means hurt them; they will lay hands on the sick, and healed they shall be; they will recover."

Verse 20 continues to tell us,

"And they went out and preached everywhere, and the Lord kept working with them and confirming the word they preached through the accompanying signs and wonders and miracles."

108

In 2 Peter 1:19 Peter states,

"We have the prophetic word made more sure."

Everyone knows that the prophetic word of old speaks about a coming Messiah. And we know that that same prophetic word speaks of the establishing of the Kingdom of our God through that Messiah. He would rule in every nation, every tribe, every tongue, and every people.

Peter says, *"We have this prophetic word made more sure!"*

That means it has come to pass, amen. It means **it is a prophetic word for which the time of its fulfillment has fully come!**

Peter says we now have the guarantee of this word! That means we are no longer sitting there with a secret in our hearts. It is time for that secret to come out. It is time to make it known.

Peter says,

"You will do well if you pay attention to this, as to a lamp shining in a dark place, so that the sun will rise in your heart. That means that that revelation will also burn in your own heart."

You see, **God will always confirm His Word!**

In Jeremiah Chapter One verse twelve, God Himself says to Jeremiah, *"I watch over My Word to perform it!"*

And in Isaiah 55:10 & 11 God spoke again and said,

*"For as the rain comes down, and the snow from heaven, and does not return there empty handed, but first waters the earth, making it sprout and bring forth a harvest, giving seed to the sower and bread for food, **so shall My Word be that goes forth from My mouth, it shall not return to Me void, but it shall accomplish its purpose, it shall prosper in the thing for which I sent it.**"*

Listen, God doesn't see needs. He is not moved by needs, He sees His Word. He is moved by His Word, He is moved by faith.

I had such a privilege, just this past week, to pray for a precious man who had such a tremendous need in his body.

Before I laid hands on him, I explained to him that it is important for us to realize that in our prayer there is no need to try and put pressure on God to perform, *because God is Love. He loves us. He loves you!*

So, we are not putting pressure upon God in our prayer, but the purpose of our laying on of hands, the purpose of our praying is putting

110

pressure on the enemy to leave and to go. And he must flee!

And as I laid hands upon him and prayed the prayer of faith, God released His power through me and healed that precious, precious man. He was so blown away that the pain was gone and that God had healed him that he started crying and then he got so excited, he started jumping up and down for joy.

Hallelujah!

Thank you Jesus!

Sometimes when we pray we think we've got to pray and pray and pray until we pray it through, until we've made such an impression upon our reluctant God that we have finally convinced Him that He has got to help us!

So our prayer is just like us saying, *'God, I'm twisting Your arm. Oh God, I'll fast and pray and cry and weep until you hear me!'*

But you see **that's the prayer of ignorance and confusion and unbelief!**

When we finally understand that He loves us, that it's His will to heal us, that it's His will to deliver us, *that it's His passionate desire to help us, that's when we open up to receive and that's when we'll see more results than ever before!*

I mean, you don't have to convince somebody that's already convinced.

You don't have to convince somebody to be willing who is already willing, amen!

Chapter 14

Get Rid of Confusion & Unbelief!

Listen, many many people forget to consider that there is another factor at play in their situation. They forget that someone else is also involved and to blame other than God.

That someone is called, *"The Thief"* who comes to steel and to destroy and to kill!

With that kind of mentality that forgets or refuses to consider the enemy's involvement or perhaps even his existence, the devil has been getting away with a lot!

Satan, the father of lies, has been lying to many *'churches'* and many believers for many years.

He has them deceived and convinced that everything that happens to you is God. Everything, it doesn't matter if it's good or if it's bad, it's God. God is sovereign, if it happens to you it is God, everything is God. So, they never resist the devil because he is not a part of their equation. They are convinced that it can't be the devil, it's God!

And so if they develop a cough or some sickness, they immediately think, *'Well, I guess it's just God teaching me to prevail. He is just working patience in me.'*

And so they just put up with the cough or the sickness or whatever, and the devil is having a good time *because nobody is resisting him!*

Because people believe that God's putting this sickness on them, and the devil has them convinced somehow, and they're deceived into believing this stuff!

But listen, if you believe that way and you go to the doctor, you are going against the will of God, aren't you? *Because God wants you sick, you see.*

Hey, don't ridicule me now or call me stupid for making this argument. It just makes logical sense doesn't it? *It's the logical end conclusion of such a belief.*

I mean, think about it: If God wants you sick and He is the One who put the sickness on you, *or allowed it to be put on you,* then ought you not to get as sick as you possibly can, *so that you can really please Him?*

114

I mean, then you might as well not go to the doctor, or take any medicine whatsoever, *otherwise you might be going against the will of God!*

In fact you ought to get good and sick, as sick as you can possibly get, and maybe you should just go ahead and die then and get it over with, *because that way you would really please God, now wouldn't you?!*

If God put that sickness on you, *or allowed it to be put on you, then your death would be the ultimate end in pleasing God, now wouldn't it?!*

I say again: If it is the will of God for you to be sick, then don't go to the doctor and don't take any medicine, *because then you are going against the will of God, if it is indeed the will of God for you to be sick.*

If it is the will of God for you to put up with your problem, *then don't resist it, because you'll be going contrary to the will of God.*

Can you hear how ignorant it sounds to believe that it's the will of God for you to put up with your problem, or for you to put up with sickness in your body?

People don't even think twice about believing these things!   They never stop to question these religious mentalities to see if it holds water.

They just believe and accept whatever garbage they are taught.

Listen, God watches *over His Word.*

We can't put any pressure upon God about anything. We can't change God. We will never be able to change the character of God. That's a good thing, *do you realize that?*

That means you will never be able to change God's opinion about anything!

Do you know what God's opinion towards sickness and disease is? He sees it as part of the curse of the fall that came upon us through Adam *and which He reversed in Christ Jesus!*

What God has to say about sickness and disease in Jesus is that *He has no part in it.*

In fact *He is against it!*

He was personally present in Christ *to come and deal with it!*

By His stripes, by Jesus' stripes, we were and therefore are healed!

That's God's opinion about sickness and disease! God's opinion towards sickness

is that *we, His children, should have no part in it.*

He doesn't want anything to do with sickness and disease, *it's a curse!*

He doesn't even want to be remotely associated with it.

And He doesn't you to associate Him with it in your mind!

He wants to bless you, amen! He wants you blessed, not cursed, amen!

Jesus said that, *"If you've seen Me, you've seen the Father!"*

Listen, Jesus didn't go around breaking people's arms and blinding people, and beating people over the head until they had a headache and saying, *'I did that because God wanted to teach you something.'*

Jesus was the greatest teacher. He lived as an expression and an extension of the ministry of the Holy Spirit and of the Father.

I remind you again of what was said in Acts 10:38,

"...God anointed Jesus of Nazareth with the Holy Spirit's power; He went about doing

*good, healing all that were oppressed by
the devil, for God was with Him."*

Jesus went about doing good, healing
everyone that was oppressed of the devil.

He exposed the works of the devil. And He
came to undo the works of the devil!

1 John 3:8 says,

*"For this purpose was the Son of God made
manifest: to destroy the works of the evil
one."*

So the Word made flesh went about
demonstrating the will of God! He came to
set the captives free!

And God hasn't changed in well over 2,000
years now, amen. Because He is not
limited to time, amen! No, listen, He is still
the same: yesterday, today, and forever!

God's attitude towards sin in your life is the
same, amen. He doesn't want it for you,
because it steals, destroys, and kills, amen.

The wages of sin are still death, amen. So
God doesn't want it for you. He doesn't
want it in your life. He wants to set you free
and save you from it, amen.

God's attitude towards sickness is the same as well, amen. He doesn't want it for you. He doesn't want it in your life, amen.

It comes to steal, destroy, and kill, and He doesn't want it for you. He doesn't want sickness to be a part of your life. He wants to set you free and save you from it, amen.

God's attitude towards these things is still the same. He will never change His mind about them, amen!

Religion has been floundering around and changing their minds on everything, every time they get challenged on anything.

Religion has been trying to be politically correct and trying to accommodate all these problems and things they seem to be powerless against and that's why they have to keep coming up with stupid arguments that don't make any sense if you just take five minutes to think it through.

It never ceases to amaze me how a bunch of sincere, but religiously ignorant and confused people, can sit around in a group, and oh, they are very sincere all right. But they are so deceived when it comes to spiritual things. They sit around and have these seemingly innocent little group discussions about, *'Why we think we should be sick,'* and they basically sit there and apologize for the Christian faith and pass of their so-called beliefs and faulty reasoning to the unsuspecting new-comers.

No wonder the world thinks God is really cruel.

'I mean, just look at that poor little baby, that baby was born cripple or with Down Syndrome or some other sickness or disease. How could God do a thing like that!'

But you see the enemy is behind it all.

He wants to reflect in people's hearts all the time a bad attitude towards God, *and he uses people's wrong religious views to reinforce it.*

He wants to build and reinforce an attitude in their hearts that says, *I can't really trust God because He is so unpredictable and so cruel. I don't know what He is going to do next. I mean, my child might just suddenly fall in the swimming pool one day when no one is around to save them and drown, or maybe some other horrible thing is going to befall me!'*

This is the attitude that has been built by the devil in people's hearts towards the character of God.

But God desires for you and for me to have life more abundantly!

How can anyone trust such a *'god'* as religion portrays, a *'god'* that is a lie, a *'god'* that gives me life but then just as easily takes it away and gives me sickness and disease and death!

James 1:17 tells us clearly *not to be deceived, for <u>every good and perfect gift comes from above</u>, from the Father of Light, with whom there is no shifting shadowiness, no variables, no dark side, no other side, no cruel side!*

So, it is such a relief to know that God is love, period. GOD IS LOVE!

It is such a relief to find out that I don't need to try and put pressure upon God through my praying. There is no need to try and put pressure upon God. GOD DOESN'T CHANGE!

My praying is simply making my request known before my Father God *who loves me.*

My praying is simply making my request known before my Daddy *with thanksgiving.*

Where does that *"thanksgiving"* come from?

The *"thanksgiving"* is my simple recognition of His provision that is already mine! So I simply thank Him when I have a need. I don't thank Him for the need. No, I thank Him in spite of the need, in the face of it.

I thank Him for His goodness and for His love that is already fully mine and for what He has already made available and given me in Christ Jesus, and I say something like, *'My precious Daddy God, I just want to voice this request...'*

You see, Paul encourages us in Philippians Chapter Four and he says,

"Do not be anxious about anything, but in everything, with prayer ...and thanksgiving, make your request known to God, and the peace of God, that passes all understanding, that peace that was given us in Christ Jesus, will guard your heart and mind..."

The enemy would want to drain my joy and my energy by having me get all anxious about my problem. But before I get all caught up in that anxiety, I am reminded of Paul's words there in Philippians and I remember his encouragement, how he said, *"Now, don't be anxious!"*

And then I nip that anxiety in the bud and I refuse to be anxious and I begin to put my trust afresh and anew in the love of my Daddy God for me.

So how can I just not be anxious? I mean how do I not get anxious?

Paul says, *"come on precious one, with prayer ...*__*with thanksgiving*__*, make your request known to God, the One who loves you intensely with an everlasting love, the One who came and demonstrated and proved His love for you in Christ Jesus beyond a shadow of a doubt!"*

He goes on to say, *"And then the peace of God will come and guard your heart and mind..."*

Why will His peace come?

His peace will come and confirm to you in your heart that He has already made provision! And then suddenly you will no longer have anxiety ruling you, but you will have peace ruling your heart and mind!

Amen!

Hallelujah!

And you see when peace rules, anxiety is out of business!

Sickness and problems and disease had its power over you through anxiety. But now you put anxiety aside, you cast it out, you expel it from you, and you throw it out the door, boots and all, and it will just have to take its sickness or its problem or its disease with it out the door, amen!

The peace of Jesus comes to rule in your heart now, because you are making your request known before your Daddy God *with thanksgiving.*

We are not beating on heaven's door and praying heaven down, and getting God to change His heart and move!

No, that's a bunch of religious nonsense!

God's already shown His heart through His Word made flesh in Jesus! God's already moved on our behalf in Jesus Christ!

Now once we fully grasp these things and take our rightful place at His right hand and we say, *'Father God, my precious Daddy who loves me so very much, I thank you that You've already made provision for my freedom. I thank you that You have made provision for whatever need I have.'* Then something begins to happen.

Then suddenly my prayers begin to be answered.

Then suddenly I begin to develop a new attitude and I turn against the enemy with authority and I tell him to get out of my body, and out of my life, and out of my family, and out of that other person's body.

Then suddenly I find myself bold enough to go around laying hands on the sick and seeing them recover, seeing them healed, seeing miracles happen right in front of my eyes!

Then suddenly I begin to take those keys of the kingdom, and God says, *'That's right My child, I have given you those keys, now go ahead and take them and use them and go and unlock those gates of hell, those gates of hades, that have kept My people, My children bound for so long. Go and bind now what's already been bound in heaven, and go and loosen now what has already been loosed in heaven!'*

Amen!

Hallelujah!

So I take that authority that has already been given me in Christ Jesus, and by the anointing of the indwelling Holy Spirit, and by faith, I now release it. I go and through faith I bind the activity of that thing in my body. Maybe it's been cancer or something, and it has been growing in my body, or in that other person's body, and it wants to take my whole life; it literally wants to take their life, amen. But now suddenly, through the faith of God quickened in me, I bind it; I put it to a stop!

That's exactly what the term *"binding"* means. It means I put a stop to whatever it is!

It's like saying, *'Satan, you have gone far enough. In fact you have gone too far already in my body, or in my neighbor's body, and I put a stop to your activity right now. I refuse to let you continue in your activity any longer, any further! I put a stop to it right now!'*

You see, that word of faith begins to speak to me. The faith of God that rises up in my heart changes my attitude towards the devil, and towards that sickness, or that disease, and it has no more room to maneuver or function any further, and it has to flee, it has to go!

Do you see how important this is?

If my attitude towards that sickness or that disease is, *'Well, maybe God is putting this on me, or putting it on my fellow man, because He is trying to teach us something, or trying to work something out of us that doesn't belong in our character,'* then there

is no way I can resist that thing with confidence.

You see, if I come to your house and I am a thief, and I intend to steal from you, but I have this uniform on that has a name tag for some local plumbing business on it, and I come to your door and I knock, and I say to you, *'I am the local plumber and the city has sent me out because there is a problem with all the plumbing in your area, and I have come to inspect your plumbing.'*

And you swallow that lie and believe me, and so you say, *'Oh welcome, isn't that great, how thoughtful of the city to send you out to my house. Please come inside, make yourself at home. I'll quickly make you a cup of tea, just to properly thank you, and give you a few cookies to eat, before you get going on the job.'*

But in the meantime I am sitting there and I am checking out your house because I want to come back and break in here tonight when you are sleeping. And here you are; I have fully convinced you that I am the plumber guy, and so you sit there and you are entertaining me, because you have been deceived by my appearance, and you think I am the official plumber guy, sent out on a special errand by authority of the city government.

Listen don't you think the devil knows that trick? He knows that if he could come

disguised as an angel of light, disguised as God Himself, disguised with God's uniform on, saying something stupid that sounds plausible, saying something like, *'Well I am just here to teach you some spiritual lesson or something. I'm just here to teach you some patience or something like that which you need you see, so I am putting this cancer on you, or this problem, or this other sickness or disease, and the next thing, and the next thing... and blah blah blah. I represent God, you see, and I'm your friend and this is good for you. It is for your good!'*

And so you think, *'Oh well, I guess I have got to make peace with it and live with it you see. I will just have to put up with it and endure it, because who can resist God, who can resist the will of a sovereign God?!'*

So you entertain this *'god'* and you put up with this thing.

But if you suddenly realize it's a lie, and that, *'Listen, this is a wolf in sheep's clothing, this is the devil himself, and he has disguised himself. He has but clothed himself in the guise of truth, just so that he can come and rob me and steal from me,'* then you immediately change your attitude from wanting to serve the devil with tea, to one of serving him with a quick uppercut to the jaw and kicking him with the left foot of fellowship, right out the door!

You see, once you discover the truth, the truth sets you free, amen!

Once you discover the true identity of your foe, you can get rid of him, amen.

And once you discover the true identity of Jesus, you discover your true identity as well! You discover that you are your Father's child, and the He loves you! You discover that you are royalty and that you have authority, amen!

I have authority over the enemy! I am not a reed, blown about by every wind of doctrine, and I'm not a wave tossed to and fro upon the seas of life by every circumstance and contrary wind that blows against me either. No, I'm a rock: steadfast and immovable, always abounding in authority, because I am abounding in the knowledge of God. I am abounding in the knowledge of my true identity as child of God. I am abounding in the love of God. I am abounding in grace and revelation and faith!

Through His Word, through revelation knowledge, through the knowledge of His love, through the knowledge of my

reconciliation, through the knowledge of redemption, God puts a rank on you, amen!

And the truth of His Word changes your mentality to accommodate that rank, amen!

I so appreciate Jesus' parable about the centurion. Listen, that guy knew what his rank was!

He didn't have to struggle with timidity, and say to those guys, *'Now, guys, would you mind doing me a big favor and going here and going there? Or, please, would you mind, doing this and doing that…'*

No, he just said, 'GO!' and they went.

He said, 'COME!' and they had to come.

All because of that authority which He represented!

God wants you to know what your rank of sonship looks like in the heavens!

He wants you to know what those keys are that He gave you, what it can do.

He wants you to know what it means to you, what it affords you to have those keys in your possession.

He wants you to know what those keys represent, so that you can, with authority, unlock that gate!

God wants you to release the captives from the prison the enemy has them bound in.

You have the keys to that gate! You have the keys to that prison! You have the keys of the kingdom, the set of master keys that unlocks every gate!

Now I know that sometimes bad things happen, and suddenly you find yourself in the middle of it, and you wonder, *'Were am I? What direction is my life going in now all of a sudden?' But then you wake up and you turn to God, and you cry out, and you are filled with trust in God, and God hears you, and God intervenes, and God turns things around and work the thing for your good, because you love Him and He loves you!*

You should go read my book, *"Fully Persuaded!"* as well, to understand this more fully!

Chapter 15

A Mobilized Church!

Let's just quickly go back to Mark 16:15,

"And Jesus said to them, 'Go into the entire world, and preach the gospel to everyone'"

He didn't say to them, 'Go into all the world, and build buildings and lock yourselves in there and wait for the rapture or the second coming or something!'

Mark 16:15 doesn't say, *'Go into the entire world, build comfortable buildings, and make sure the people are really comfortable so that the 'church' can grow to at least 3000 or so. And don't keep them too long in the services because, you know, human nature being what it is, I don't want you to lose those people. So make it really comfortable for them, and really go out of your way to cater to their soul, and build these monstrosities and lock yourselves in there, and just wait for Me. I will come back. In fact, I will come one day when you least expect it. Oh, and don't worry, if you pray hard enough, I will hear from way up in heaven, and come visit you down here with revivals every now and then, or often enough, and I will come down and heal your land.'*

No He didn't say that!

He said,

"Go into all the world and preach the gospel to everyone, to the whole wide world, and he who believes, that means, he who responds to your preaching and embraces My message, the truth of My gospel, the truth of their reconciliation to Me, and their sonship restored, is immersed; identifying themselves with My salvation, that person shall be saved…"

"And these signs will accompany those who believe: In My name, they will speak with new tongues. In My name they will cast out devils …and in My name they will lay hands on the sick and they will recover!"

I am just letting you have a look at HIS 'CHURCH', because GOD is building HIS 'CHURCH', amen.

And God's *'building'* is not that largest building with the highest tower and the nicest carpet and the nicest seats that *we have in mind.*

No, but His *'building'* is a *'building'* with power! Amen!

God's *'building'*, God's *'church'*, is that place, that people, that body of believers, where His Word, His revelation, His gospel is confirmed with signs and wonders following!

He says, *"In My name they will cast out demons…"*

Hey that sounds to me like *"binding"*.

In other words, the devil is lose among that bunch of people in that community and he was doing his thing, and suddenly here comes the Lord's *'church'* into that community and preaches the truth of the gospel and takes authority over those devils and kicks them out!

Just recently, we had a most wonderful time in a small little town somewhere out in the country not too far from where we live. We took a whole team of disciples with us, our whole ministry team, and I tell you what, when we as the *'church'* showed up there, the power of God manifested.

The people that came from that community and attended the meeting could hardly stay seated in their chairs, or even stand on their feet for that matter under the power of God. People were crying and weeping; they were just beside themselves.

We saw healings manifest before our eyes, and we saw revelation knowledge just break forth into people's hearts, hardened religious people, their resistance broken down under the power of the Spirit. We saw the power of God manifest, because when the Word of God, the true gospel is introduced, when light comes into darkness, darkness cannot even put up a flight. It just flees, amen, it flees!

And this is exactly what Jesus is talking about here in Mark 16:15.

Jesus says,

*"If you go, and preach …if you go **and proclaim** the good news, the gospel, do it boldly, do it with confidence, with faith, with persuasion and conviction, do it in clarity and purity, and simplicity!"*

Before you can perform the miracle, quite often *something must be proclaimed first* to challenge those demons, to challenge those strongholds in that person's thinking and in their lives.

***Something must be proclaimed* so that faith can come.**

Everywhere in the ministry of Jesus you'll find Him teaching and preaching and healing, and quite often, in that order and not the other way around.

Not that He couldn't just go around healing people. He often did that too.

Besides, the dead do not have ears to listen to anything you say; *they don't have faith,* amen. If anything is going to happen there it sure isn't going to be because the dead person listened and believed, amen. It is because you believe!

But, I want you see that, most of the time in Jesus' ministry, that is what He did, He went around teaching and preaching and healing, and that was His custom, He did it, in that order.

He would lay a foundation in teaching and preaching. He would boldly and confidently declare the truth of the gospel, from the Scripture, and then He knew His Father watches over His own Word spoken by the lips of Jesus, watching over that Word to perform it.

Jesus understood the importance of that truth foundation. He knows, once I have laid that foundation in truth, God My Father watches over His Word to perform His

Word, to make His Word good, and it will happen!

He didn't wonder if it would happen, amen.

No, *He knew it would!* Amen!

But Jesus didn't just cling to His ministry as if it was His exclusively, as if no one else was allowed to function in that ministry of the Father, that ministry of the Holy Spirit, that ministry of proclaiming the truth of the gospel and watching God watch over His Word and perform it and confirm it with signs and wonders following.

No, Jesus sent others out. He sent out the twelve, and then sent out the seventy others also, and before His death He plainly told them that, *"As the Father has sent me, so send I you!"*

He said, *"Everyone who believes in Me, the same works that I do they shall do also and greater works than these shall they do!"*

Jesus sent His disciples out and He is sending us out also, and He is saying, *'Go and proclaim what you have heard and believed and experience. Go and proclaim it, and then watch me confirm that proclamation with signs and wonders, because of the faith of God stirred up in*

138

you and released in them that hear you preach!'

Now it doesn't help to proclaim a watered down, inferior version, a compromised version of the gospel. No, we must proclaim the gospel in such a way that many believe!

You see, there is a lot of other preaching going on, but it is in such a way that many doubt and end up even more confused.

We can preach in such a way that many feel tickled in their ears, with a word that lines up with their crooked thinking, with a word that agrees with their unbelief, with a word that sounds so good and so eloquent, but has no substance to it.

And they will come up afterwards and pat us on the back and say, *'Oh wasn't that just lovely? I enjoyed your talk, you did such a good job, I felt so entertained.'* **But they go away with nothing. And nothing in their thinking, nothing in their understanding, nothing in their faith was challenged!**

Listen, we must preach in such a way that many are persuaded, in such a way that many believe!

Why?

So that through their faith the door can be opened for the Holy Spirit of God to confirm His Word with power!

So, *"Go into the entire world, preach this gospel to everyone, and these signs will follow…"*

The devil is having a heyday **but,** *"Cast out demons, heal the sick, cleanse the lepers, raise the dead!"*

Jesus said, *"Freely you have received, now freely give!"*

"Cast out demons!"

Say to them, *'You will no longer continue to torment this person's mind with your depression, and with your lies and fears and anxiety and whatever! I break your power, and I cast you out!'*

'You will no longer be allowed to torment this person in their body, either. I cast you out!'

These signs will follow, amen.

"You will lay your hands upon the sick and they will recover."

Because you have now preached the Word, and this sick person, it doesn't matter, he or she may have been sick all their lives

perhaps, but they heard what you preached, and now they say to themselves, *'Well, I believe.'*

The foundation was laid in truth, revelation knowledge broke through, *"upon this rock I will build My 'church'."*

So the revelation comes into that person's heart, faith came into that person's heart, and the foundation is laid for that person to receive their healing.

But now the symptoms are still sitting there you see; the gates of hell are still standing there. But now Jesus says, *"Upon this Rock I will build My 'church' and the gates of hell will not prevail."*

That means it will not be superior in strength, but the revelation will break through, it will be superior, it will totally break through that mentality that has made room for that disease to hold on with such tenaciousness. It will break through the power of that sickness, *to release the captive.*

And that person sits there and they have heard the truth, and a foundation was laid for their healing, and revelation broke through, and they say to themselves, *'I believe.'* And they allow you to lay your hands on them, and they are totally open and receptive and persuaded that God will honor His Word, and so the power of God flows and the miracle happens *and they are healed!*

In the laying on of hands, I am not releasing some magical kind of power. I am not waving some magical *'Harry Potter wand.'* No, but *it is just a point of contact.*

And I am saying, *'Father God here is a person who believes. Here is a person in whose heart the gospel has found a home. Here is a person in whose heart the revelation of Christ is born. And as I am laying my hands upon this person right now, I am also extending my faith; I am also believing. Father God and I am using the keys of the kingdom of heaven right now. I am exercising the authority You gave me. I bind the activity of this disease in this person's body. I bind the intention and the purpose of darkness to destroy this life in this body, to destroy this person!'*

You see, I lay my hands to confirm these things.

And the sick will recover.

They will recover.

That means that sickness will be undone, it will be gone, that power will be broken, and that person will be restored.

Can you see God's method in His strategy for His *'church'*?

He wants to see a whole people, a free people, a released people, *a people of power.*

Okay, let's just finish up there in Mark 16.

So, after the Lord Jesus had spoken these things He was taken up into heaven.

What a disappointment.

I mean, if He could have just stayed, if they could have just somehow convinced Him to stay on the earth with them, then they could have just continued to watch Him doing it.

And sadly, that has been the mentality of the *'church'*, even in our day.

'Well, Todd Bentley, TB Joshua, or whomever it is these days, when are you coming to our town again sir, so we can watch you do it?'

'When is God going to send Uebert Angel to America, so we can watch him do it?'

'When is God going to raise up somebody like TB Joshua over here, so we can watch him do it?'

That's been the mentality of the *'Church'* here in America and everywhere. All the while Jesus has been proclaiming for years, ***"Go in this thy might! Isn't it I that sends you!"***

Jesus has been proclaiming for years, *"The **WORD** is near <u>you</u>, in <u>your</u> heart and in <u>your</u> mouth!"* (Romans 10:8)

Can you imagine the impact on your town or on your region, or on this nation and the other nations of this world, if all of a sudden the *'church'* would start operating in the anointing of this *'Word,'* this true gospel, this revelation of Jesus Christ and the successful work of redemption.

And listen to me now, the anointing is not some weird power that we get or that comes upon us out of nowhere sometimes if we're fortunate.

No. The anointing is God recognizing the faith of God when He sees it coming alive in you. The anointing is the grace of God in action.

The anointing is when God confirms His Word, when God recognizes your faith in the integrity of His Word.

And you go and you pray and it happens, because you put your faith in God, and in His power, and you come to the realization,

144

'I am not a building, I am a person, and God can use me. I've got hands, I've got feet, I've got a mouth, I can speak words; I can speak in line with the 'Word!'"

It might come out awkward and not so eloquent, but the spirit truth still comes forth and God's Spirit is all over it and liberates people that are in bondage!

But many believers just sit there and they wonder, *'Now when am I ever going to be used? Maybe they will ask me to come and help clean up afterwards.'*

And that's all fine and good, let's all clean up and all the other things that need to get done. ***BUT the unction that God has in mind for His body is to liberate the prisoners!***

And now I can just hear someone say in their heart already, *'Oh man, this Rudi fellow, he just wants to turn the whole 'church' into evangelists.'*

Well amen, brethren, let the chips fall where they may, **because God's vision for His 'church' is to evangelize.** *And not in the way that we used to look at evangelism, amen,* **but we are all called to function in the anointing of the Holy Spirit in sharing and proclaiming the gospel with confidence and boldness, and to set the captives free in** that same anointing and power of the indwelling Holy Spirit.

God's anointing is in the evangelist as an individual, but it is in that individual as part of the ingredient in the body of Christ necessary to equip the saints for the work of the ministry.

God never called an individual evangelist to go and evangelize. He called the *'church'* to evangelize!

God wants to use anointed individuals to release the truth of the gospel accurately, which releases the evangelistic anointing within His body, *within the 'church', within the saints, for the saints to do the work of the ministry.*

And when we look at the ministry, when we look at the word, 'ministry', when we look at the ministry of Jesus as a whole, when we look at that ministry of the Spirit, when we look at what 'ministry' is, and we study it, we will find that *there really is only one 'ministry' given to all of us.* And that is *"the ministry of reconciliation"* we read about in 2 Corinthians 5:14-21.

Of course, a portion of that ministry, is everything and everyone, the whole body, busy nourishing the body, and feeding the body to sustain the body and keep the body encouraged and fully engaged in the life of Jesus.

But this is, so that the real work of the ministry can be accomplished through the body: the work of reconciliation, of setting the captives free and immersing them in Christ, connecting them to Him and to the rest of the body, the *'church',* the family and household and dwelling place of God.

It says there in Mark 16:15 that, *"These signs will accompany those who believe."*

Notice: *"...**those who believe**."*

We cannot expect the signs and the supernatural to just be there automatically. The supernatural doesn't get released until something is released in someone's heart first.

That something is called revelation knowledge; it is called faith, God's faith, amen.

"So then, the Lord Jesus after He had spoken these things to them was taken up into heaven..."

It wasn't a disappointment, amen, *because He already placed the revelation and the anointing and the commission within them.*

They knew they now had to go, per His instruction, and wait in Jerusalem and the power would come and they would go. And the end of Mark there, tells us the rest of the story, in a brief statement.

It says, *"And they went forth and preached everywhere, while the Lord worked with them, confirming His Word with signs and wonders and miracles."*

Now notice: *"…while the Lord worked with them."*

'Huh? I thought He was taken up into heaven.'

I have news for you: **So are we. We are seated with Him in heavenly places, in Christ Jesus.**

You see, our concept of heaven needs to change. Our concept of heaven in our Sunday school mentality is maybe some remote place on some unknown planet in outer space somewhere, or something like that.

Jesus said, *"**Behold, I will be with you always, even until the end of time!**"*

And here we are and we think, *'I wonder how long it's going to take for me to get to Him, or for Him to get to me.'*

Listen, that heavenly realm is much closer than you think, than what many of you can even imagine... ha... ha... ha...

We have been restricted for so long by our senses. We have been restricted to see only as far as our natural sense of sight permits us to see. But listen; **there is another realm, a realm more real, more eternal, more permanent than this natural realm that fades away.**

We have obtained that eternal position. In Christ Jesus, we have obtained access to that realm through revelation knowledge, through the revelation revealed in Jesus Christ.

And now we obtain that position and we bring it into the now, because we wrestle not against flesh and blood, but against principalities and powers in heavenly places.

The heavenlies: heavenly places is that unseen realm of reality, that unseen realm of spirit truth, that unseen spirit realm of spirit realities.

We are involved in spirit dimension realties.

It is a spirit-war that we wage. The weapons we use to make war with, the weapons of our warfare are not natural.

BUT they are mighty in God, they are powerful beyond compare. They are spiritual. Those devils are no match for us. With the sword of the spirit, with the very words of our mouth, and with the power of God behind our words, and within us, we are speaking and declaring and we are laying our hands on people, and we are releasing that power, and we are pulling down those strongholds that have people bound! (Those demonic strongholds in people's bodies and minds, those spiritual strongholds inside of people; those strongholds of thinking, those demonic strongholds of lies and deception and vain imaginations and philosophies and theories, man-made ideas that try to exalt themselves as truth, that try to exalt themselves against the knowledge of Christ, against the knowledge of the gospel, against the knowledge of a complete redemption!)

So, when I speak the words of Jesus, when I speak the truth of the gospel, whether I feel the goose bumps or not, I know that I am speaking integrity. I am speaking spirit truth, and I know God watches over that, God watches over His Word to perform it, so I am going to watch with Him. I'm going to say, *'Alright God, now I've put Your Word out there, and now I stand back and I watch, now You go ahead Father and do what You do best. You perform Your Word. You confirm Your Word with signs following. You heal the sick, You do the miracles, It's all You Jesus! I just speak the Word, I just lay my hands, but it's You who does it!'*

What's in the hands? It's not in the hands, amen.

There is something *in our hearts,* so our hands or our clothing or our shadow, even and our mouths, could be an extension of *what is in our hearts!*

"Such as I have, give I unto you!"

"In the Name of Jesus Christ, GET UP AND WALK! In the Name of Jesus Christ, you devils COME OUT! In the name of Jesus Christ SEE, or HEAR, or BE HEALED! ...or whatever!"

"And the Lord worked with them, and confirming His Word, with the signs, and the wonders, and the miracles that attended it."

In closing, I urge you to get yourself a copy of *The Mirror Bible.* It is the best translation of the Scriptures from the original Greek that I have ever read, and it's available online at: www.friendsofthemirror.com or at www.amazon.com and several other book sellers.

If you want me or someone from of our team to come to where you are, *anywhere in the world,* and give a talk or teach you and some of your friends *about the gospel message and these redemption realities,* simply contact us at www.livingwordintl.com

Or you can always find me on Facebook.
If your life has changed as a result of reading this book, *please write to me and let me know.*

I would love to share in your joy *so that my joy in writing this book may be full!*

That which was from the beginning,

which we have heard
(with our spiritual ears),
which we have seen
(with our spiritual eyes),
which we have looked upon
(beheld, focused our attention upon),
and which our hands have also handled
(which we have also experienced),

concerning the Word of life,

we declare to you,

that you also may have this
fellowship **with us;**

and truly our fellowship is with
the Father
and with His Son Jesus Christ.

And these things we write to you
that your joy may be full.
— 1 John 1:1-4

About the Author

Rudi & Carmen Louw together oversee and pastor Living Word International.

They also travel and minister both locally and internationally.

Rudi was born and raised in the country of South Africa, while Carmen grew up in Cortland, New York. They function in the ministry of reconciliation (2 Corinthians 5:18-21) and flow strongly in the gifts of the Holy Spirit and His anointing to teach, preach, prophesy, heal, and whatever is needed to touch people's lives with the reality of God's love and power.

God has given them keen insight into what He has to say to mankind in the work of redemption concerning the revelation and restoration of humanity's true identity.

Therefore they emphasize THE GOSPEL: IN CHRIST REALITIES, the GRACE of God, the WORD OF RIGHTEOUSNESS, *and all such eternal truths essential to salvation and living the CHRIST-LIFE.*

They have been granted this wisdom and revelation into the knowledge of God by the resurrected Spirit of Jesus Christ, *to establish and strengthen believers in the faith of God, and to activate them in ministering to others.*

Not only are people set free from the poison and bondage of sin, condemnation and all kinds of intimidation, (upheld, strengthened and reinforced by age old religious ideas born out of ignorance) **but many are brought into a closer more intimate relationship with Father God, as Daddy**, through accurate teaching and unveiling of the gospel message, prophetic words, healings and miracles.

Rudi & Carmen are closely knitted together with many other effective Christians, church fellowships, and groups of believers who share the same revelation and passion.

50407734R00087

Made in the USA
Charleston, SC
23 December 2015